The Yachtsman
Skye & Northwe

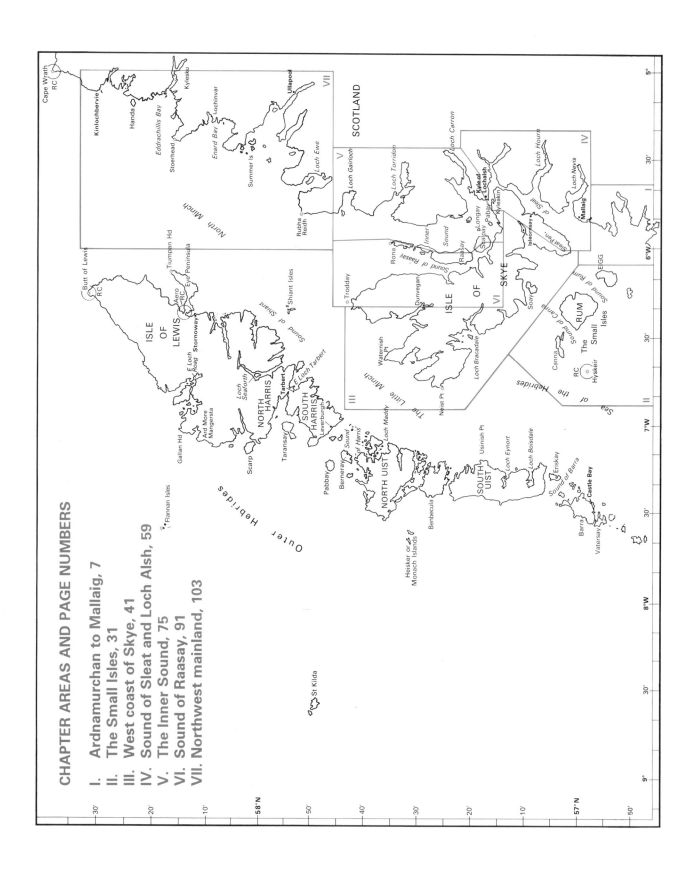

CHAPTER AREAS AND PAGE NUMBERS

The Yachtsman's Pilot to Skye & Northwest Scotland

MARTIN LAWRENCE

Imray Laurie Norie & Wilson Ltd
St Ives Cambridgeshire England

Published by
Imray, Laurie, Norie & Wilson Ltd
Wych House, St Ives, Huntingdon,
Cambridgeshire PE17 4BT, England
☎ +44 (0) 1480 462114 *Fax* +44 (0) 1480 496109
1997

ISBN 0 85288 368 4

British Library Cataloguing in Publication Data.
A catalogue record for this book is available from the
British Library.

PLANS
The plans in this guide are not to be used for
navigation. They are designed to support the text
and should at all times be used with navigational
charts.

CAUTION
Every effort has been made to ensure the accuracy of
this book. It contains selected information and thus
is not definitive and does not include all known
information on the subject in hand; this is
particularly relevant to the plans, which should not
be used for navigation. The author believes that its
selection is a useful aid to prudent navigation, but
the safety of a vessel depends ultimately on the
judgement of the navigator, who should assess all
information, published or unpublished.

CORRECTIONS
The editors would be glad to receive any corrections, information or suggestions which readers may
consider would improve the book, as new im-
pressions will be required from time to time. Letters
should be addressed to the Editor, *The Yachtsman's
Pilot to Skye and Northwest Scotland*, care of the
publishers. The more precise the information the
better, but even partial or doubtful information is
helpful, if it is made clear what the doubts are.

CORRECTIONAL SUPPLEMENTS
Imray pilot books are amended at intervals by the
issue of correctional supplements. Supplements, if
available, are supplied free of charge with the books
when they are purchased. Further supplements are
available from the publishers. The following should
be quoted:

1. Name of book
2. Date of edition (above)
3. Date of last supplement (if applicable)
4. Name and address to which supplement should
   be sent, on a stamped addressed A4 envelope.

The last input of technical information was March
1997

Printed in Great Britain by Bath Press Colour Books
Ltd, Blantyre, Scotland

Contents

Preface

The first volume of the first part of this series of *Yachtsman's Pilots* for the West Coast of Scotland was published ten years ago. The third volume, *Castle Bay to Cape Wrath*, covered the Outer Hebrides and Skye and the northwest mainland. With new developments, new information and the addition of colour photos, that volume developed a kind of middle-age spread, and it seemed appropriate to divide it in two. This makes the process of revision more digestible as well as relating each part to a different local authority, on whose officers I rely closely for information.

I have taken the opportunity to rationalise the different volumes by incorporating parts of *Crinan to Canna* into this volume.

Some plans have been added, by scanning large-scale Admiralty charts from the last century and the different graphics emphasise that these are based on old data.

This is unlikely to be the first volume of the series to come to the reader's notice, so its history need not be repeated here. While I have sailed on the West Coast for nearly 30 years I make no claim to personal knowledge of every anchorage described, and my purpose is to gather information from every available source and present it in the clearest possible way. There are many people who know far more about individual areas than I do, and some of them have generously given me the benefit of their experience and taken a great deal of time to discuss their observations.

It is the constant complaint of writers of pilot books, whether published commercially or by clubs, that they receive little support from users. Thus, I would urge any yachtsman who knows of uncharted hazards or information which would be of value to other small boat users, to supply the fullest details to the Hydrographic Office. The Office relies heavily on information from users, particularly for less-frequented areas such as these, and is not sufficiently well funded to be able to update its surveys except for some very pressing commercial or military purpose.

The photographs used here have been chosen as far as possible to supplement the charts and plans. Ideally, photos should be taken at low spring tides to reveal as many hazards as possible. Printing these photos in colour often shows more detail than is possible in monochrome. However it takes many years to visit each place at a specific time of day and month, whether by sea, land or air – with no guarantee that conditions will be suitable for photography when one gets there, so that coverage isn't as comprehensive, and some of the photos not as clear, as I would like. I have also used photos taken by other yachtsmen.

Acknowledgements

Margaret Wilkes and the staff of the Map Room of the National Library of Scotland have been patiently dealing with my requests for obscure information for many years. I am particularly grateful to the following for information for this edition: John Armitage, Robert Arnold, Tony Barry, Mike Bolton, Jim Ferguson, Nigel Gardner, Rob Martin, Philip Pendred, Richard Scholes and members of the British Gas Sailing Club, John Shepherd, Norman and Gillian Smith, Major B E Sykes and Rob Teago.

Imray's editors meticulously checked every detail, and the final form of the plans is due to Imray's cartographers, working from the outline drawings which I provided.

The publishers are grateful to Elizabeth Cook who compiled the index.

Author's note

Many of the plans in this book are based on British Admiralty charts with the permission of the Hydrographer of the Navy and the sanction of HM Stationery Office but, above and beyond that, I am extremely grateful to the Hydrographer and many of his staff who have taken time to search through archives and reply to requests for information.

There is much that is not fully known about parts of the West Coast and, in spite of checking by many people, it cannot be certain that all errors have been eliminated. The fact that an anchorage or passage is described is no guarantee that it is usable by you on the day you are there. There could well be hazards which I have missed by luck rather than good management and, in spite of all the efforts of Imray's staff and others, there may be simple errors which have been overlooked – even the supplements to the *Admiralty Pilot* contain the occasional comment 'for E read W'! Scepticism and checking against all other information available is the safest course to adopt.... with any directions.

Before following the directions, plot the course on a large-scale chart and, if you are confident that any errors will not be fatal, proceed. If you disagree with what I have written, or find mistakes or changes, then please let me know, through the publishers.

Martin Lawrence
Mid Calder
1997

Introduction

The area described in this volume lies within a rectangle 100 miles by 50, equivalent to the English Channel between the Solent and the Straits of Dover, or the southern North Sea between Ramsgate and Cromer.

North of Ardnamurchan the scale of the landscape is, for the most part, more dramatic, and there are fewer of the intimate anchorages associated with the southern part of the West Coast. There are some extremely well-sheltered anchorages, but many of these will give you anxious moments before you are safely inside.

It may be significant that there are no castles or castle ruins on the mainland coast of Loch Carron, implying that there was nothing there worth defending. Almost the only way this area related to the outside world was through the Jacobite adventures of 1745.

There are many islands, many inlets, no marinas, almost no commercial harbours, few services and supplies, and fewer organised entertainments, but the natives are friendly. Daylight in summer is longer than in the Channel, being 400–500 miles further north, and the weather is less settled on the whole. But, if you are prepared for the conditions which this paragraph merely hints at, you may experience unique and memorable cruising. The whole area, however, is increasingly at risk from fish farming, and future oil development.

Throughout the northwest Highlands, Skye and other islands there is excellent climbing and hillwalking, and a small boat provides unique opportunities to combine climbing and sailing.

This pilot sets out to provide as much information as may be useful to small-boat visitors to the waters of northwest Scotland, clearly and concisely. The upper limit of size for which the book is intended is a draught of 2 metres, and it includes information applicable to shoal-draught boats – centreboarders, trailer-sailers, twin-keel boats and multihulls, and motor cruisers. In many anchorages there are parts which are only accessible to shoal-draught boats, particularly those which can dry out fairly upright.

However, while the smallest boats, even cruising dinghies, may be at home in much of the area described in this pilot, they must be soundly equipped and competently handled by experienced crews.

The West Coast is no place for anyone who is unable to deal with adverse conditions which may arise unexpectedly. A good way to gain experience of the West Coast is to take a berth on one of the skippered charter yachts or instructional courses which are available. Some of the waters covered by this volume are sheltered by islands or are within lochs which penetrate far among some of the highest hills in Britain. This shelter creates problems of its own, particularly the squalls which are generated in the lee of hills as well as the higher rainfall. Anyone who is capable of managing a yacht at a comparable distance from the shore whether in the North Sea, the Baltic, the English Channel, the Atlantic Coast of France or the Irish Sea should have little problem on the West Coast of Scotland. However, the lack of navigational marks (and the number of unmarked rocks), and the strong tides in some passages will require some adjustment on the part of the navigator. To set against these are the relative absence of commercial shipping and also the visibility which is usually good – except in rain; fog as such is fairly rare. To complete a round of generalisations, the climate is wetter and cooler than, for example, the south coast of England (although the further west you go, out of the lee of the hills, the drier the weather), but a compensating factor is the longer daylight in summer, so that you rarely need to sail at night.

Equipment should be as robust and reliable as for a yacht going a similar distance offshore anywhere in the English Channel or the North Sea, and a more comprehensive stock of spare parts carried, owing to the remoteness from sources of supply.

Anchors

So many yachts are now kept in marinas and only sail to another marina, or to a harbour, that anchoring is no longer an everyday operation but, on the West Coast, it is essential that the crew is thoroughly familiar with anchor handling. You should have at least two anchors, of the sizes recommended by anchor manufacturers or independent reference books, rather than those supplied as standard by boat builders which are often on the light side. Chain rather than rope will restrain a yacht from roving around in gusts, but if you do use rope it will help to have an 'angel' (a weight which can be let down to the seabed on a traveller). Whatever the design of the anchor there is no substitute for weight and I suspect that the reputation some anchorages have for poor holding may be rather more due to many yachts having inadequate anchors. Attention should be devoted to ease of handling; unless you stick to places with visitors' moorings (and there's no guarantee that one will be free) you will be using the anchor frequently.

Drying area at the head of Loch Sheildag. The heads of lochs dry out, anything up to half a mile

Chartering

Charter boats are available, both for bareboat and skippered charters, within the area of this volume from Armadale in Skye and Badachro by Gairloch, as well as from further south. Many of the operators are members of Associated Scottish Yacht Charterers, whose brochure can be obtained from Sail Scotland Ltd, 7 Alexandra Parade, Dunoon PA23 8AB *Fax* 01369 705588. Other tourist information may be obtained from the Scottish Tourist Board, 23 Ravelston Terrace, Edinburgh EH4 3EU ☎ 0131 332 2433.

Charts

Imray's charts *C65*, *C66* and *C67* at 1:150,000 give better coverage for passage making than any current Admiralty charts and are more convenient to use.

Between Ardnamurchan and the north of Skye and Loch Gairloch the four Admiralty charts *2207–2210* (1:50,000) are essential. There are no larger-scale charts between Ardnamurchan and Mallaig and the south side of Skye.

Further north, the scale of chart you choose depends on the degree of intricate pilotage in which you intend to indulge. Probably you will need some larger-scale charts (around 1:25,000) together with either the Imray charts or Admiralty charts *1785, 1794* and *1795* at 1:100,000.

Get your charts early so that you have time to order more, if it looks as though your first choice is not enough.

Some obsolete charts show more detail than any current one and sometimes at a larger scale, but the soundings are in feet and fathoms. They should of course only be used to supplement current charts, not as a substitute for them; although it has been observed that 'rocks don't move', new hazards are discovered (sometimes the hard way), buoys are moved around, and new features are constructed.

The Clyde Cruising Club (CCC) publishes a folio of sketch charts which may be found convenient although they show less detail than the Admiralty charts.

Maps published by Ordnance Survey at 1:50,000 or Bartholomew at 1:100,000 provide more topographical detail than current hydrographic charts (see Appendix II). Where the charts are at a small scale the Ordnance Survey maps may also be some help for navigation.

Travel

Transport There are good roads to those places on the mainland coast where one might make crew changes, although they are often narrow and patience needs to be exercised with touring coaches, caravans and heavy lorries.

Car ferries to Skye run from Mallaig to Armadale and the new bridge from Kyle of Lochalsh to Skye (although the tolls have been set at a level to reward a speculative builder rather than as a public utility).

Trains to Mallaig run from Glasgow via Fort William, and to Kyle of Lochalsh from Inverness.

A variety of long-distance and local bus services reach most places . . . eventually.

A combined timetable for all transport in the Highland area, which was sponsored by government agencies, has been discontinued.

Trailed boats may be launched at Arisaig, which is a few miles south of Mallaig. Plockton, Gairloch, Kylesku and, for Arisaig, phone Arisaig Marine ☎ 01689 450224; the others are public facilities.

Passage making

Unless you are crossing the Minch the distance between the entrances of sheltered anchorages is rarely more than 12 miles.

Serious navigation is still necessary but, for much of the time, it is a matter of pilotage by eye and satisfying yourself that what you see corresponds to the chart.

The most useful position lines are transits such as tangents of islands, or beacons in line with headlands and these should be picked out on the chart in advance.

Compass bearings should, of course, be taken as well, if only to avoid wrongly identifying a whole group of islands.

At night salient points and hazards in the Minches, Sound of Sleat and Inner Sound, and in the approaches to lochs and inlets used by naval and commercial traffic, are well enough lit but in these latitudes there is little darkness in the summer months.

Radiobeacons are located at Stornoway (aero), Butt of Lewis and Cape Wrath. Details are given in the appropriate chapters.

Visibility is commonly good and fog as such is rare. The *Admiralty Pilot* says that 'visibility of less than ½ mile may reach 3 days per month in midsummer' and visibility of less than 2 miles 'does not average more than 3 days per month during the worst summer weather at Stornoway and Tiree'.

Lobster and prawn creel floats are often encountered even in the middle of the Minch and in the fairway of approaches to anchorages. Often, floating lines lie upstream of the float, especially at low tide, and sometimes stray lines lie downstream.

Weather

Weather is extremely variable and any statistics can be interpreted so widely as to be of little help. After visibility the aspects of most concern are wind speed and direction, and rainfall.

Rainfall is greatly affected by the proximity to high ground, and annual figures vary from less than 1,000mm at Arisaig to between 1,250 and 1,800mm in the Sound of Sleat and Inner Sound, and between 2,300 and 3,000mm at the heads of Lochs Hourn, Nevis and Torridon.

Broadcast forecasting schedules vary from year to year and a current almanac should be consulted. Apart from the shipping forecasts on BBC Radio 4 and inshore waters forecasts on Radio 3, general weather forecasts are often equally relevant where land and sea are so much intermingled.

Marinecall inshore weather forecasts are currently broadcast on VHF Ch 67 by Oban Coastguard at (or soon after) 0240, 0640, 0840, 1040, 1440, 1840, 2240 and by Stornoway Coastguard at 0110, 0510, 0910, 1310, 1710, 2110 (local time).

MetFax services may be obtained from those hotels catering for yachtsmen and from harbourmasters.

Tides

The spring range varies from 4·2 to 4·9 metres. Tidal streams are strong wherever the movement of a large body of water is constricted by narrows, and there are often overfalls at the seaward end of narrow passages, particularly with wind against tide. Overfalls also occur off many headlands, and eddies are formed, usually downtide of a promontory or islet or even a submerged reef, but sometimes in a bay uptide of the obstruction. There are also usually overfalls wherever two tidal streams meet.

Anchorages

A few very general observations may be helpful. Steep high ground to windward is unlikely to provide good shelter – in fresh winds there may be turbulent gusts on the lee side, or the wind may be deflected to blow from a completely different direction, or funnel down a valley. After a hot windless day there may be a strong katabatic wind down the slope, usually in the early morning – such conditions are by no means unknown in Scotland. Trees to windward will absorb a lot of wind and provide good shelter.

Within some anchorages there are often several suitable berths, depending on conditions, and it may not be practicable to describe them all, nor to mark each one on the plans. In any case, an anchorage suitable for a shoal-draught boat 6 metres long may be inaccessible to a 15-metre yacht with a draught of 2 metres, and a berth which would give shelter for the larger yacht might be uncomfortably exposed for the smaller.

Rivers, burns and streams generally carry down debris, often leaving a shallow or drying bank of stones, sand or silt, over which the unwary may swing – frequently in the middle of the night. The heads of lochs and inlets commonly dry off for more than ½ mile.

Within any anchorage the quality of the bottom may vary greatly. Mud is common (usually where there is little current), but its density may not be consistent and there are likely to be patches of rock, boulders and stones; also clay which tends to break out suddenly. Sand is also common, but sometimes it is so hard that an anchor, particularly a light one, will not dig in. Weed of all kinds appears to be on the increase, but it does vary from year to year.

Fish farms are increasing at an alarming rate, usually outwith the most popular places, but attempts are sometimes made to establish them in recognised anchorages as well. There are two main forms: cages for 'fin fish' (usually salmon), and rows of buoys from which ropes are suspended, on which shellfish are 'grown'. These buoys may have ropes between them on or close to the surface. Fish cages may be moved around within a bay or inlet, often because they have

created so much pollution that the fish can no longer live in the original location, so that they may not be found where shown on a chart or plan. The boundary of an area licensed for fish farming is sometimes marked by buoys, usually yellow and sometimes lit. These are often a long way from the cages, and there may or may not be moorings or other obstructions within the area marked out by the buoys.

Beacons are often not at the extreme end of the hazard which they mark.

Car ferries run to very tight schedules and the space to manoeuvre at a ferry terminal is often restricted. Yachts must leave clear turning space near ferry terminals; apart from the safety aspect they may be disturbed by the wash from a ferry's bow thruster. Ferry schedules differ from day to day and Caledonian MacBrayne's current timetable (easily obtained from tourist offices and ferry offices or by post from Caledonian MacBrayne Ltd, The Ferry Terminal, Gourock PA19 1QP) is useful to avoid conflict in the often very constricted space around terminals.

Moorings for fishing boats are laid in many anchorages, but many are not used in summer as their owners are often working on the Atlantic coast of the Outer Hebrides, and you may be invited to use a fisherman's mooring. Do not pick up a buoy unless you are sure that it is a mooring buoy and not marking creels for storing live prawns – or another yacht's anchor buoy!

Visitors' moorings are provided by local hotels free of charge to yachts whose crews patronise their establishments, as well as by the HIE (Highlands and Islands Enterprise, formerly Highlands and Islands Development Board). They are arranged (as they have to be) to suit the largest boats likely to use them, and of course, a boat on a mooring behaves differently from a boat at anchor. The effect can be to reduce, rather than increase, the number of visiting boats that can use an anchorage. There is no guarantee that the mooring is suitable for any boat intending to use it.

Visitors' moorings have been laid in several locations to attract more business to local traders. These moorings have large blue buoys marked 'HIDB visitors 15 tons'. There is no pick-up, and a rope has to be fed through a ring on top of the buoy. If your bow is so high that the buoy is out of reach and you cannot pass your rope through the ring, the best way to secure to one of these moorings is to lead a rope from the bow to the lowest point amidships, pick up the buoy there and take the end of the rope back to the bow. Two turns should be taken round the ring, and an appropriate knot formed to avoid the chafe which would occur with a slip rope. The practice of rafting up together on these moorings is not now encouraged.

John Macrae, the harbourmaster at Kyle, is co-ordinating the provision of improved facilities for yachts throughout the northwest and welcomes both queries and comments from users (☎ and *Fax* 01599 534167).

Quays, piers, jetties, slips, linkspans and related structures are in need of some definition, as the categories overlap and a structure identified on the chart may have fallen into disuse, or been replaced by one of a different type, or have a description well above its status. The following definitions are used in this book, to give some indication of what you may expect to find.

A *quay*, *wharf* or *pier* is used by fishing boats and occasional coasters, and usually has at least 2 metres of water at its head at chart datum. It is often constructed of piles or open framing, or stone or concrete with vertical timber fendering, alongside which it is difficult for a small yacht to lie without a robust fender board. A pier projects from the shore, but a quay or wharf is either part of a harbour or parallel to the shore. Many of these structures were erected or extended by the Admiralty 40–50 years ago and some which have not been maintained are in very poor condition.

Ferry terminals serving the Outer Hebrides all have a *linkspan* for a bow-loading car ferry. The inner end is hinged and the outer end, supported between concrete towers, is raised or lowered to match the height of the ramp on the ferry, according to the state of the tide. The linkspan is usually at one end of a quay alongside which the ferry lies.

A *jetty* is smaller and, for yachts, more user-friendly but often dries alongside. Newer jetties are constructed of more or less smooth concrete, older ones of stone, often with a very uneven surface; a few are of timber.

A *slip* runs down at an angle into the water, although its outer end may be above water at low tide and it may be used by a ferry to an inshore island. There is sometimes sufficient depth for a yacht to go alongside a slip for a brief visit ashore for stores.

With the enormous growth in inshore fishing and fish-farming many of these structures are in regular use by fishermen whose livelihood depends on being able to land their produce quickly, and yachts should take care not to obstruct them.

Dues are charged at some piers and harbours, even for a brief visit to take on water. While this may be seen as one way in which yachtsmen can contribute to the local economy, the charges sometimes appear disproportionate to the service obtained. The Highland Council is introducing a 'season ticket' to enable yachtsmen to use facilities at several harbours for a single payment.

Facilities

Considerable time, resourcefulness and imagination need to be devoted to obtaining supplies or services but local people are, as it were, in the same boat and usually go out of their way to be helpful. Ferrymen, piermasters, hotel keepers, postmistresses and fishermen are all willing and useful sources of information, and there are many services and sources of supply that are too irregular or ephemeral or unknown to be listed here.

There are few yachting services as such, although yacht chandlers at Badachro, Ullapool and Portree will advise.

Sailing clubs exist at Plockton, Gairloch and Ullapool.

Caley Marine at Inverness, ☎ 01463 236539, operates a mobile repair service.

Showers or baths are often available at hotels. Mobile banks operate widely throughout the Highlands and Islands. Bicycles are available for hire at Lochboisdale, Lochmaddy, Castlebay and Kyle.

Diesel is often more easily available by hose in small fishing harbours, but do not expect quick service; fuel is supplied to yachts as a favour, although usually very willingly, but the person dispensing it may have better things to do than turn out to supply a relatively small quantity.

Water supplies at the quayside are fairly rare, and a yacht with built-in tanks should have a portable container or two, together with a straight-sided funnel, with which to fill the tank. A 20-metre hose of the flat variety on a reel, with a universal coupling to fit on any sort of tap is also well worth carrying, as several small jetties have taps but no hoses. These small jetties, although they may only be approachable above half tide, are usually more convenient than the massive piled ferry piers, where the only hose may be too large to serve a yacht.

Eating ashore A reasonably varied selection of eating places is scattered throughout the area, one or two aspiring to gourmet status, and many at which you will eat well if unadventurously, whether in a restaurant or a bar. No recommendations are made as establishments can change hands, and standards, rapidly.

Communications

Phone boxes are fairly well distributed and are referred to where known, but the 'rationalisation' of the telephone service may lead to a reduction in their numbers.

Post offices Many now have very restricted hours of opening.

VHF radiotelephones The mountainous nature of this coast puts some areas out of range of either the coastguard or coast radio stations. The east side of Skye, for instance, is a blind spot for making link calls as the transmitter is on the west side.

Emergencies

Serious and immediate emergencies (including medical ones) are usually best referred to the coastguard. If you don't have VHF R/T but are able to get ashore (for example, if a crew member is ill), phone the coastguard or police. For less serious problems, such as a mechanical breakdown out of range of a boatyard, mechanics experienced at least with tractor or fishing-boat engines, will often be found locally.

Coastguard The Maritime Rescue Sub Centres for the area are at Oban ☎ 01631 563720 and Stornoway ☎ 01851 702013.

Lifeboats are stationed, within the limits of this volume, at Mallaig and Loch Inver and, further afield, at Oban, Castlebay and Stornoway.

Notes on plans and pilotage directions

Generally the conventions used on Admiralty charts have been followed so that this pilot may be used in conjunction with them. See also *Charts* on page 2.

In each chapter, information about charts, tides, dangers and marks, relevant to the whole, comes first; then any passage directions, sometimes including certain anchorages where it is necessary to relate these to plans associated with the passages; then any branches from the main passage; and finally individual anchorages, usually in the same sequence as the passages described.

Conspicuous features are listed to help identification in poor visibility.

Lights, and any directions for making a passage or approach by night, are separated from the description of dangers and marks, as most of us sail mainly by day, and this reduces the amount of information to be absorbed.

Bearings are from seaward and refer to true north. A few of the plans are not orientated with north at the top in order to make the best use of the space available, but reference to the north point on the plan will make this clear.

Distances are given in nautical miles and cables (tenths of a nautical mile); a distance of less than ¼ cable is generally expressed in metres.

Co-ordinates to locate anchorages are approximate. Except where stated, these are not waypoints.

Depths and heights are given in metres to correspond with current Admiralty charts.

Depths are related to the current chart datum which is generally lower than that on older charts. It is the lowest level to which the surface of the sea is expected to fall owing to astronomical causes. If high barometric pressure and/or strong offshore winds coincide with a low spring tide the water may fall below this level, in which case there will be less depth than shown on the chart or sketch plan.

Tides Heights of tides are represented by five sets of figures; these are: mean high water springs (MHWS), mean high water neaps (MHWN), mean tide level (MTL), mean low water neaps (MLWN), mean low water springs (MLWS).

The word 'mean' is important because (for example) low water springs in any particular fortnight may be substantially higher or lower than the mean.

If you have tide tables which give heights of tides at Ullapool you will be able to relate the tide on any particular day to the equivalent figures there (5·2 3·9 3·0 2·1 0·7) and judge whether the rise and fall will be greater or less than the mean.

The difference between times of tides at Ullapool and Dover may vary by as much as 40 minutes, so that tide tables for Ullapool will give more accurate results than those for Dover. Tide tables for Ullapool are included in all almanacs but are not published separately; but the constant for that port is +0110 relative to Oban, for which a booklet of tables is widely available.

The Simpson Lawrence *Yachtsman's Almanac – North and West Britain*, published annually, is available from chandlers or by post from the publishers: Clyde Marine Press, Westgate, Toward, Argyll PA23 7UA.

Shelter The heading 'Shelter' at the beginning of each chapter implies an anchorage for which to run in reasonable visibility if the wind is increasing.

Place names are a frequent source of confusion and there may be differences between the name used on a current chart, on an older chart, by local people and by yachtsmen. Anglicisations or translations are sometimes used quite arbitrarily on current charts among a nest of Gaelic names. The name on the current chart (or in the absence of a name on the chart, the OS map) is always given in this pilot, together with a popular name if the chart name is unpronounceable.

As place names often need to be spoken the following approximate pronunciation of common words in names may be helpful:

Bagh   Bay
Bogha   Bo'
Caol   Kyle
Caolas Kyles
Dubh   Doo
Mhor   Vore
Rubha   Ru'

Names of lochs, etc, are normally written as two words (Loch Inver, for example), but the name of a settlement beside the loch as a single word (Lochinver).

Photographs and views from sea level are used to illustrate transits and clearing marks, or to help identify landmarks, while air and hilltop photos often show more detail than can be included in the plans. Transits are, in some cases, more clearly illustrated when the marks used are not actually aligned; where this is done the marks are indicated by pointers.

KEY TO SYMBOLS

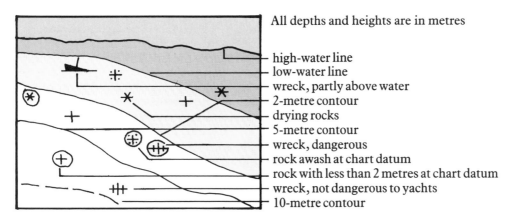

All depths and heights are in metres

- high-water line
- low-water line
- wreck, partly above water
- 2-metre contour
- drying rocks
- 5-metre contour
- wreck, dangerous
- rock awash at chart datum
- rock with less than 2 metres at chart datum
- wreck, not dangerous to yachts
- 10-metre contour

I. Ardnamurchan to Mallaig

It used to be customary for any yacht returning from a cruise beyond Ardnamurchan to display a bunch of heather at the end of her bowsprit as a token of having been round this exposed headland. Ardnamurchan is a key point in any cruise on the West Coast, partly because of the exposure, but mainly by contrast with the sheltered waters of the Sound of Mull.

The Point itself has none of the hazards associated with headlands such as Portland Bill or Land's End; there are no offlying rocks or shoals, nor strong tides, but the bottom is uneven and beating against such tide as there is can be very unpleasant.

As the prevailing wind is from the southwest these conditions are most likely to arise on your way home, and this possibility should be allowed for when planning a cruise.

After a yacht has rounded Ardnamurchan the passage NNE gradually takes her into more sheltered water towards the Sound of Sleat, but rocks, both marked and unmarked, lie as much as a couple of miles offshore.

Tidal streams run at up to 4 knots in places with relatively shoal banks which can cause an unpleasant sea. It can be difficult to find the way in to most of the lochs between Ardnamurchan and Mallaig, but some of them are outstandingly attractive and well worth the effort.

The north side of the Ardnamurchan peninsula has no shelter, except in moderate offshore winds in Loch Ceann Traigh (Kentra) at its east end, and there are several dangerous rocks along this shore.

Loch Moidart, between the Ardnamurchan peninsula and the major inlet of the Sound of Arisaig, is very difficult to enter.

The Sound of Arisaig itself divides into Loch Ailort and Loch nan Uamh, both of which involve intricate pilotage but, in the mouth of Loch Ailort, there is an island behind which it is feasible to run for shelter given reasonable visibility.

North of Rubh' Arisaig on the north side of the Sound of Arisaig is Loch nan Ceall (Arisaig Harbour), entrance to which would be almost impossible without the beacons erected by the yacht centre there. Note that Arisaig Harbour and the Sound of Arisaig are entirely separate places.

Mallaig, towards the entrance of the Sound of Sleat, is a busy fishing and ferry harbour, fairly easily entered by day or night, good for supplies. The harbour is currently being extended and when the work is completed there should be more space for yachts.

Charts

The only relevant Admiralty chart is *2207* at a scale of 1:50,000, but its northern margin is a mile short of Mallaig. Chart *2208* will probably be needed for the continuation northward in any case. Imray's chart *C65* extends to Mallaig.

Tides

Off Ardnamurchan, the flood stream runs northeastwards, and the spring rate is 1½ knots. On the ebb an eddy sets inshore south of the point. Heavy seas build up with onshore winds, especially with wind against tide, and it is best to keep 2 miles off the point.

Between Eigg and the mainland tidal streams run as follows:

The NE-going stream begins +0550 Ullapool (+0130 Dover)

The SW-going stream begins −0010 Ullapool (−0430 Dover).

The maximum rate is generally 1 knot but, near the east shore of Eigg, the rate is up to 4 knots; in the bight between the north side of Ardnamurchan and Rubh' Arisaig the rate is negligible.

Dangers and marks

The lighthouse at Ardnamurchan is very conspicuous but, if approaching from the Sound of Mull, it is not visible until it bears 001°.

Bo Kora Ben, a submerged rock with a least depth of 1·8 metres, lies 6 cables NNE of Ardnamurchan lighthouse and 2 cables offshore.

Bo Faskadale, a group of drying and submerged rocks 6 miles northeast of Ardnamurchan lighthouse and more than 2 miles offshore is marked on its northwest side by a green conical light buoy which is often difficult to identify if there is any sea running.

The only other artificial mark is the white light beacon on Eilean Chathastail at the southeast point of Eigg.

Off the Arisaig promontory, on the mainland east of Eigg; rocks above water and drying extend more than half a mile from the shore and, further north, many drying rocks lie more than a mile from the shore.

Several banks, although more than 14 metres below chart datum, cause very heavy seas, particularly with wind against tide.

The two most significant are Maxwell Bank, about a mile across, 1 mile southeast of Eigg, and Oberon Bank which is small in extent, 3 miles east of the point of Eigg.

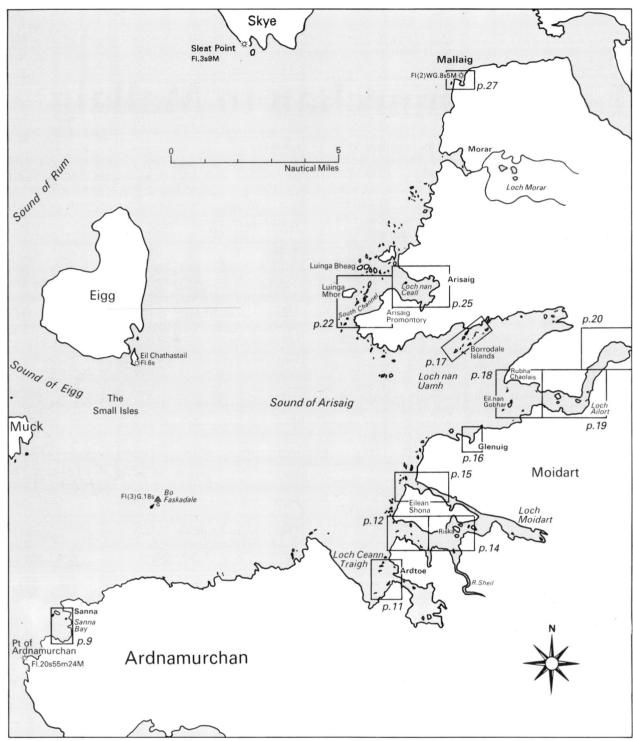

A local magnetic anomaly is charted east of Muck and south of Eigg. Another has been noted two miles south of Muck.

Passage notes

Waypoint 2 miles west of Ardnamurchan 56°43'·5N 6°17'W

Waypoint ¼ mile northwest of Bo Faskadale 56°47'·7N 6°17'·0W

The passage from Ardnamurchan NNE towards the Sound of Sleat is straightforward enough in clear, moderate weather.

From a point 2 miles off Ardnamurchan steer 037° to pass east of Eigg.

To avoid Maxwell Bank, alter course more to the east, not less than 070°, when Bo Faskadale buoy has been identified, or when the southwest side of Rum comes open north of Muck bearing 322°.

Heading south or southwest, particularly from Arisaig, tend towards Muck and Eigg until Bo Faskadale buoy is identified.

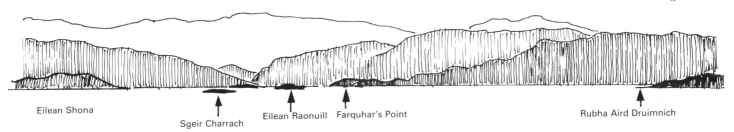

Eilean Shona   Sgeir Charrach   Eilean Raonuill   Farquhar's Point   Rubha Aird Druimnich

North side of Ardnamurchan

Waypoint ¼ mile north of Sgeir Charrach 56°47'·7N 6°17'·0W

The passage along the north side of Ardnamurchan has two dangers which are fairly easily avoided although there are no specific clearing marks.

Elizabeth Rock with a least depth of 0·7 metre, lies 1 mile south of Bo Faskadale buoy and 1¼ miles offshore.

Sgeir Charrach which dries 2·6 metres (at approximately half-tide), lies ¼ mile off Rubha Aird Druimnich which is the most northerly point on the peninsula. Look out for Bo Ruadh, awash, 4 cables ESE of Sgeir Charrach.

Soundings are very irregular here and give no guide to position. Steer to keep Rubha Aird Druimnich bearing 083° until Bo Faskadale buoy is abaft the beam, then steer to keep the south point of the Sound of Arisaig, Rubh' a' Phuill Bhig, bearing not less than 060°, to clear Sgeir Charrach.

Lights

At night the following lights (in clear weather, as they are a long way apart) make a direct passage between Ardnamurchan and the Sound of Sleat reasonably straightforward.

Ardnamurchan lighthouse Fl.20s55m24M
Eilean Chathastail, southeast of Eigg, Fl.6s24m8M
Bo Faskadale buoy Fl(3)G.18s
Sleat Point light beacon Fl.3s20m9M

The harbour at Mallaig is well lit, but there are no lights at any anchorage.

Anchorages

Sanna Bay

Waypoint south of Sgeir Horsgate 56°44'·6N 6°12'W

A delightful sandy bay 1½ miles northeast of Ardnamurchan lighthouse, sheltered to some extent by a reef projecting from its southwest side, Sanna Bay should probably be treated as only an occasional anchorage.

From the south the bay immediately north of the lighthouse might be mistaken for Sanna Bay and from the north, White Sand Bay, which lies east of Sanna Point, might be taken for it.

Meall Sanna behind Sanna Bay is the highest land on this part of the coast; apart from this the bay can only be identified by reference to the lighthouse and Sanna Point, north of which the coast falls away to the east.

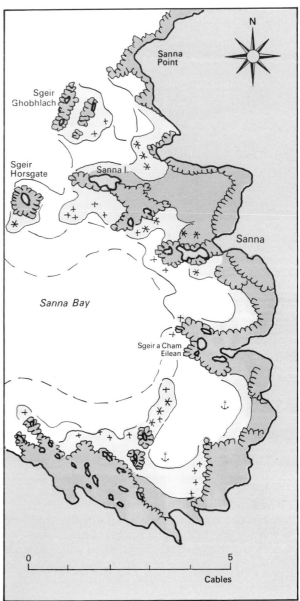

Sanna

Tides

Constant at Loch Moidart -0048 Ullapool (-0508 Dover)

Height in metres at Loch Moidart

MHWS	MHWN	MTL	MLWN	MLWS
4·8	3·5	2·6	1·6	0·5

Dangers

Bo Kora Ben, a submerged rock, 1·8 metres, lies halfway between the lighthouse and the south point of Sanna Bay, 2 cables off the north point of the bay to the south of Sanna Bay.

9

Sanna Bay from the south. Part of the reef is uncovered.

The detached cottage on the south shore of Sanna Bay (left of centre).

To the north of Sanna Bay drying rocks extend ¼ mile WSW of Sanna Point.

A reef, parts of which dry, extends at least two-thirds of the way across the mouth of the southeast part of the bay from its southwest side.

Even on the quietest day there is often a swell running into the bay, and the marks by which to avoid the reef are not easy to identify.

Approach and anchorages

From south keep at least ¼ mile offshore until Sanna Bay is well open, to avoid Bo Kora Ben.

Steer towards Sgeir Horsgate on the north side of the bay and approach as from the north (see below) to be sure of avoiding the reef.

From north pass at least ¼ mile off Sanna Point, and southwest of Sgeir Horsgate.

Steer for the more southerly of two white sandy beaches ahead, below the south peak of Meall Sanna, bearing 110° to 120° (depending on how close you are to Sgeir Horsgate).

Pass about ½ cable south of the rocky peninsula, Sgeir a' Cham Eilean, and for a short visit if there is little swell, anchor off the beach ahead.

To reach the inner anchorage, when about two-thirds of the way along the detached part of Sgeir a' Cham Eilean, turn to head about 204° towards a detached white cottage on the southeast shore with a stone barn to the left of it.

On a clear day the view over the Small Isles from Meall Sanna will make the climb well worthwhile.

No supplies. Phone box at south side of the bay.

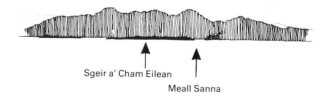

Sgeir a' Cham Eilean

Meall Sanna

Loch Ceann Traigh (Kentra)

A bay 1½ miles wide and 1½ miles deep at the east end of the Ardnamurchan peninsula, open to the north but providing occasional anchorage in offshore winds off sandy beaches at the south end. Fish cages are moored at the head of the bay.

Approach

From west follow the directions on page 9 for the north side of Ardnamurchan and, after clearing Sgeir Charrach, keep at least ½ mile off the east side of Rubha Aird Druimnich to avoid Bo Ruadh.

From north pass west of Sgeir an Eididh (11 metres high) off the east side of the bay and keep it in line with Rubh' Arisaig astern 353° to avoid a submerged rock, 1·3 metres, ¼ mile south of it.

Anchorage

Anchor in about 5 metres, south of Dubh Sgeir (1 metre high) towards the south end of the loch.

Caolas Ardtoe

A narrow inlet on the east side of Loch Ceann Traigh, ½ mile southeast of Sgeir an Eididh, leading to Kentra Bay which completely dries.

There appears to be reasonable anchorage in the narrows in 3 metres, sand, but the tide runs quite strongly through the channel, to and from Kentra Bay.

Approach

Steer ESE towards Rubha Lingan at the north side of the entrance and keep ¼ cable from that side until the entrance narrows, to avoid drying rocks extending from the south side of the entrance.

Anchorage

Either 1 cable WNW of the islet which lies ½ mile ESE of Rubha Lingan, or ½ cable south of it.

Shoal-draught boats can take the ground on sand off the stone slip ¼ mile further southeast on the north side of the inlet (any yacht with a reasonably

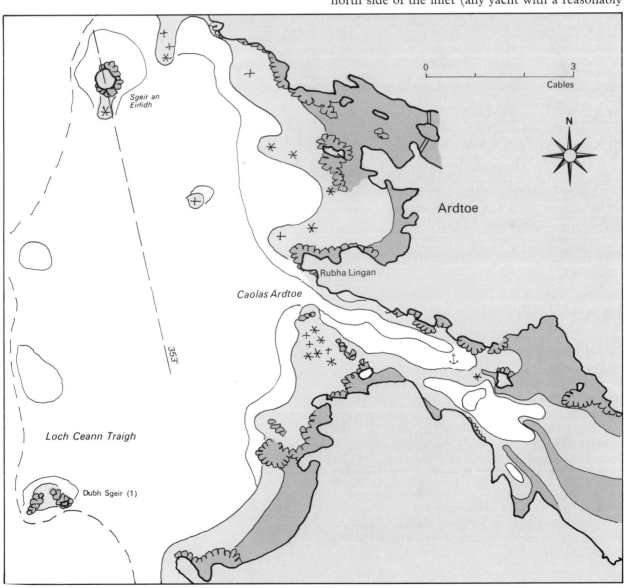

Caolas Ardtoe

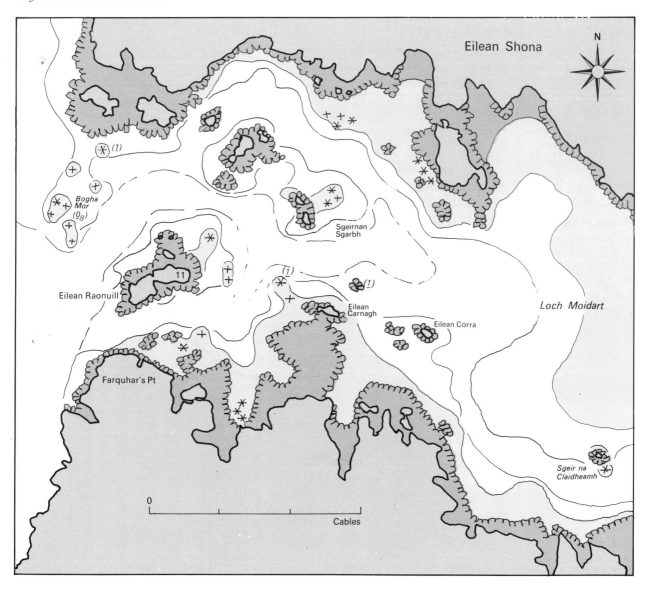

long keel could dry out alongside for repairs if necessary).

Loch Moidart

Waypoint west of Eilean Raonuill 56°47'·2N 5°53'·5W

One of the most picturesque of all West Coast lochs with sandy beaches between rocky headlands and, further in, a ruined castle on a tidal islet with thickly wooded shores on either side.

It is however one of the most difficult of all lochs to enter with a labyrinth of islets and rocks, many of them submerged or drying, and the courses to be taken on transits of islets have to be quickly identified in turn.

A steep sea builds up in the entrance when the ebb is running against a westerly wind, which is particularly likely to trouble a small yacht when leaving the loch.

The entrance lies 3 miles SSW of the south point of the Sound of Arisaig and 2½ miles east of Rubha Aird Druimnich.

Eilean Shona on the north side of the entrance is 263 metres high and merges with the hills behind it; it is easy to mistake either the North Channel or Caolas Ardtoe for the main entrance to Loch Moidart.

Charts

There is no current detailed chart of Loch Moidart. Photocopies of the very old chart *531* (see Appendix I) will provide more detail than anything currently published, subject to the usual reservations about obsolete charts.

Tides

Constant -0048 Ullapool (-0508 Dover)

Height in metres

MHWS	MHWN	MTL	MLWN	MLW
4·8	3·5	2·6	1·6	0·5

Loch Moidart approach. Eilean Raonuill stands on the right
with a pole at the highest point of the right-hand end. Castle
Tioram stands to the left of its north end. To clear the rocks
north of the fairway, the castle should be hidden behind the
island

Loch Moidart entrance – looking ESE from the passage north of Eilean Raonuill. Castle Tioram shows over the point of Shona on the left; the
drying rock northeast of Eilean Raonuill is right of centre, with Eilean Corra beyond and to the right of it.

Loch Moidart entrance, from close southeast of Sgeir nan Sgarbh. Eilean Corra is left of centre, with Sgeir na Claidheamh beyond and to the left
of it.

Approaching Castle Tioram in Loch Moidart

Approach

From the west as for north side of Ardnamurchan (see page 9); Rubha Aird Druimnich bearing 263° astern will lead direct to the entrance.

From the north keep clear west of Howorth Rock which has a least depth of 1·9 metres, ¾ mile off the middle of the west side of Shona, unless you are satisfied that there is no swell and there is sufficient height of tide for your draught. The 20-metre contour is a safe guide here.

Eilean Raonuill in the middle of the entrance, 11 metres high with a thin perch on its summit, must be positively identified.

Castle Tioram, 2 miles further east, hidden behind Eilean Raonuill bearing 094° leads south of rocks on the north side of the passage northwest of Raonuill.

Eilean Raonuill can be passed on either side but the north side is the most straightforward.

To pass north of Eilean Raonuill steer northeast to

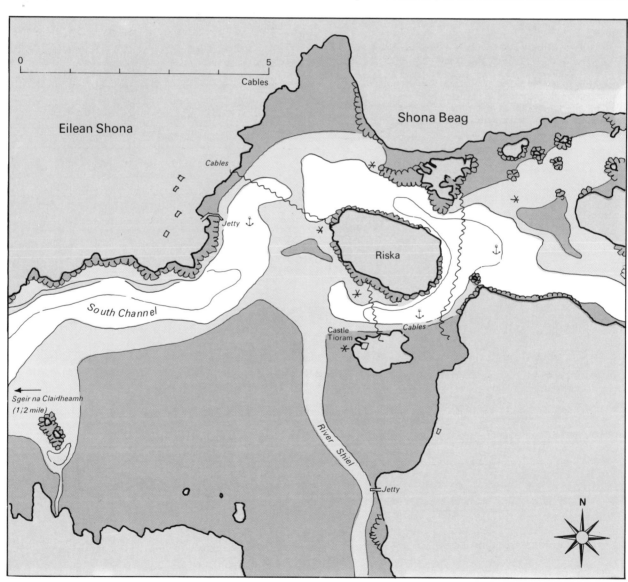

Loch Moidart

pass ¼ cable north of rocks above water on a drying reef on the north side of Eilean Raonuill.

When the east end of Eilean Raonuill is abeam head for Sgeir nan Sgarbh, a prominent rock above water 1¾ cables ENE of Eilean Raonuill, in line with the south point of Shona 097°, then pass ¼ cable south of Sgeir nan Sgarbh.

Identify Eilean Corra and Sgeir na Claidheamh (pronounced approximately as 'clay') to the southeast and when Sgeir na Claidheamh is open east of Eilean Corra, turn to pass east of Eilean Corra and ½ cable south of Sgeir na Claidheamh to avoid a detached drying rock.

The deep-water channel is quite narrow and rocks, some of which are uncharted, lie close on either side of it. A reef has been 'found' extending south from Shona in the area between the two plans in this book. The depth must be closely watched to avoid straying out of the channel. On leaving the loch, if Sgeir na Claidheadh is not immediately identified, steer 235° to pick it up.

The passage south of Eilean Raonuill is narrower than that to the north, with more dangers.

Approach the centre of the passage heading 073° to avoid a drying reef off the southwest point of the island and drying rocks east of Farquhar's Point.

Identify Eilean Carnagh and Eilean Corra ESE and, when they are in line, steer for the south point of Sgeir nan Sgarbh and then proceed as in the last paragraph above.

Several temporary anchorages can be found here but more satisfactory ones lie further in.

To continue further up the loch, approach to within about a cable of Shona.

Close west of Riska a shallow bar of sand crosses the loch, and underwater cables cross the loch both east and west of Riska; their landing places are unmarked.

Anchorages
See colour photo facing page 27

The most straightforward is ½ cable east of the jetty on Shona but this is quite exposed in southerly winds, particularly at HW.

East of Riska, a cable northeast of a rock above water off the south point of the loch there.

South of Riska, off the east end of the castle island.

If approaching from the west note that the sand bar is shallower southwest of Riska than northwest, and there are drying rocks off the southwest side of Riska.

In all cases take great care to avoid the lines of cables. Each of these anchorages is subject to fairly strong tides.

Further east most of the loch dries, with a narrow channel following the south shore. It can be explored with a dinghy or shoal-draught boat with the aid of the old chart *531*.

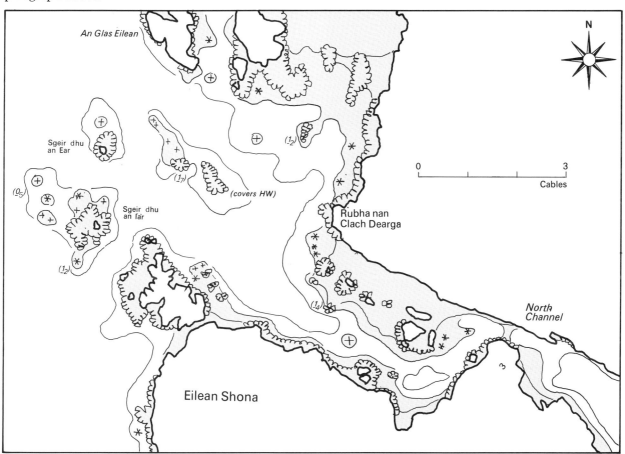

Loch Moidart North Channel

Supplies

The nearest stores are at Acharacle, more than 2 miles by the road south of the castle. Phone box ½ mile along the same road.

Castle Tioram is well worth a visit; note that the spit joining the island to the mainland covers at HW.

Loch Moidart, north channel

56°48'N 5°52'W
See colour photo facing page 27.

The main difficulty here is to identify correctly the rocks at the entrance.

Pass between the two Sgeir dhu's (their suffixes mean 'east' and 'west' although they are north and south of each other) heading for an islet close to the south shore.

Thereafter keep in the middle of the channel, but closer to the south side as the bar is approached.

The bar has a depth of 1·8 metres and the tide runs strongly over it. Anchor as far up the inner basin as depth allows.

A drying bank prevents access to the main part of Loch Moidart except for dinghies and very shallow-draught boats at HW.

If there is any sea running, entering, and particularly leaving, this anchorage could be a matter of some anxiety.

Sound of Arisaig

56°51'N 5°52'W

This is the main inlet on this part of the coast with an entrance two miles wide between Rubh' a' Phuill Bhig on its south side and a group of islets near the Arisaig Promontory on the north side. The south shore is clean outwith a cable from the shore, but there are many rocks above and below water up to a mile off the north side.

Tides

Constant -0048 Ullapool (-0508 Dover)
Height in metres

MHWS	MHWN	MTL	MLWN	MLWS
4·8	3·5	2·6	1·6	0·5

Streams within the Sound are generally weak.

Approach

Eilean an t-Snidhe, 10 metres high, lying 1 mile south of the Arisaig promontory must be identified.

Pass at least ½ mile south of that island to avoid various submerged rocks.

To pass north of this group keep the north end of Eigg, bearing 300°, just open of Eilean a' Ghaill, which lies off the Arisaig promontory, north of Eilean an t-Snidhe.

Gulnare Rock, at a depth of 2·7 metres, lies a mile east of Eilean an t-Snidhe, and Astly Rock, least depth 0·9 metres, lies 1½ cables south of the Borrodale Islands.

Both of these are avoided by keeping the north end of Muck open south of Eilean an t-Snidhe 265°.

Priest Rock off the mouth of Loch Ailort is cleared on its west side by keeping the summit of Sidhean Mor, the highest hill on the north side of the sound, open west of the end of Ardnish Peninsula on the north side of Loch Ailort 031°.

Anchorages in the outer part of the sound

Glenuig Bay (56°50'N 5°49'W), 1¼ miles east of Rubh' a' Phuill Bhig, provides some shelter but the rocks in the mouth of the bay all cover and do not provide much protection from any sea from the west or northwest.

Two perches mark rocks on either side of a passage south of the west rock.

There are several moorings in the bay, and the jetty is used by a ferry to Eigg. Anchor between the jetty and the west rock, clear of the approach to the jetty.

Hotel, shop, *Calor Gas* 1 mile up the glen. Phone box.

On the north side of the sound several inlets provide occasional anchorages, in particular Port nam Murrach, Port a' Bhathaich, and Port Doire na Drise. The approach to each of them is straightforward with chart *2207*.

See colour photo facing page 90 and between pages 58 and 59.

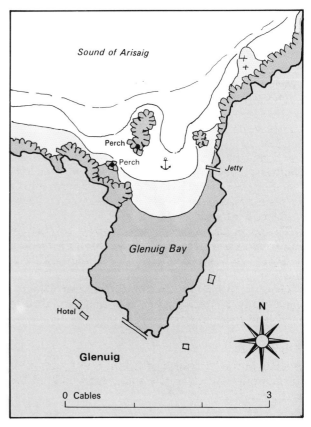

Glenuig Bay

Glenuig Bay from west.

Borrodale Islands

56°53'N 5°49'W
See colour photo between pages 58 and 59.

A string of islands on the north side of the sound providing some, although not complete, shelter.

The best anchorage is at Druimindarroch at the north end of the group, easily identified by a large conspicuous house.

Eilean nan Cabar is identified by six pine trees on its summit, and white sandy beaches on the southeast side of Rudh' Aird Mhor show up clearly.

Rafter's Reef, which dries, extends almost halfway across the passage north of Eilean nan Cabar (Cabar is Gaelic for 'rafter').

The anchorage is best approached by the north of Eilean nan Cabar, as a perch which formerly marked a drying rock southwest of Eilean nan Cabar is missing.

Give the northwest end of Eilean nan Cabar a good berth and keep closer to the mainland than to the island to avoid Rafter's Reef.

Anchorage

Anchor in the bay north of Eilean nan Cabar clear of moorings and clear of a submerged rock off the east point of the bay.

Loch nan Uamh

56°53'N 5°46'W

At the head of the loch (56°53'·5N 5°44'W) there is a deep anchorage on the east side of Eilean Gobhlach or, in southerly winds, on the north side of Ard nan Buth.

The pool east of Eilean a' Phuill may be entered by keeping towards the east side to avoid a drying rock in the middle of the entrance.

Loch Ailort

Waypoint 2 cables south of Sgeir Ghlas 56°50'·6N 5°47'·2W
See colour photo facing page 58.

The outer part of the loch is fairly open, but Eilean nan Gobhar (Goat Island) and Eilean a' Chaolais at the mouth of the loch provide some shelter and the outer anchorages are quite easy to approach.

There are quite heavy overfalls around the islands when the ebb tide runs against a strong westerly wind.

Winds between south and east produce heavy squalls from the mountains.

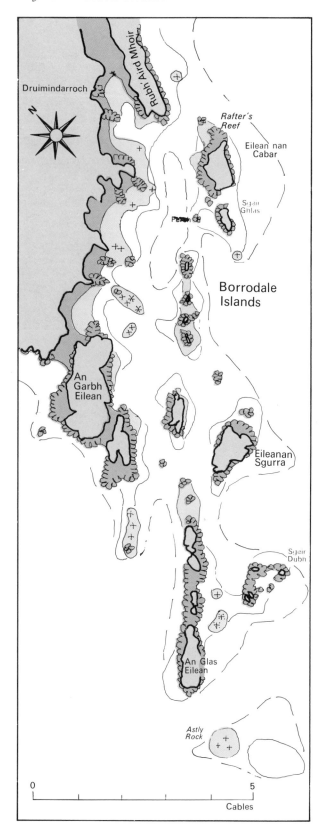

Borrodale Islands. Note: this plan is not aligned on the meridian.

Navigation of the middle part of Loch Ailort is as difficult as any in this chapter, with the usual crop of drying rocks, and islets which are difficult to identify.

Beyond the narrows, 2½ miles from the entrance, mountains close in on either side.

Dangers and approach

Priest Rock, 4 cables WNW of Goat Island, dries 1·4 metres and there is no good clearing mark for it. In the passage north of Goat Island, a submerged rock lies ½ cable north of the island.

The most straightforward entrance is by the south of Goat Island. Keep at least a cable south of the island to avoid drying rocks south and southeast of it.

The narrow passage north of Eilean a' Chaolais may be used in quiet weather, but note drying rocks up to a cable northeast of the island.

Anchorages

Goat Island (Eilean nan Gobhar) provides the best shelter in westerly winds, off a stony beach on its east side.

This is traditionally regarded as the most suitable anchorage to run for in heavy weather, although it would be unlikely to be comfortable.

The wind funnels through a gap in the middle of the island.

A submerged rock lies ½ cable off the south end of the pebble beach.

Eilean a' Chaolais, close east of the island.

A drying rock southeast of the island is cleared by keeping Sgeir Ghlas touching the west side of Goat Island.

In quiet weather anchor anywhere in the bight northeast of the island, but note drying rocks up to a cable northeast of the island.

Irens Bay off Roshven House on the south shore. Suitable in light offshore winds; anchor well offshore, between Sgeir na Sgairbh and the northeast point of the bay, as it is very shoal.

Loch Ailort, middle part

56°51'N 5°44'W

The pilotage here is less alarming than Loch Moidart or Loch nan Ceall, only because the islands in the mouth of the loch provide some shelter.

About ¾ mile east of Goat Island the loch narrows to ⅓ mile wide. The south side of the channel is shoal and drying, with rocks drying 0·5 metre about mid-channel. Eilean a' Bhuic lies west of the north point of the entrance to this channel.

Near the north shore, Bogha Sruth Mor and Bogha Sruth Beg cover about half-tide. Bo Sruth Mor to the north is slightly higher than Bo Sruth Beg.

In the next mile the channel twists between shoals and drying rocks.

Loch nan Uamh – Eilean a' Phuill anchorage from the east. Eilean Gobhlach is beyond the drying rock in the middle of the entrance to the pool.

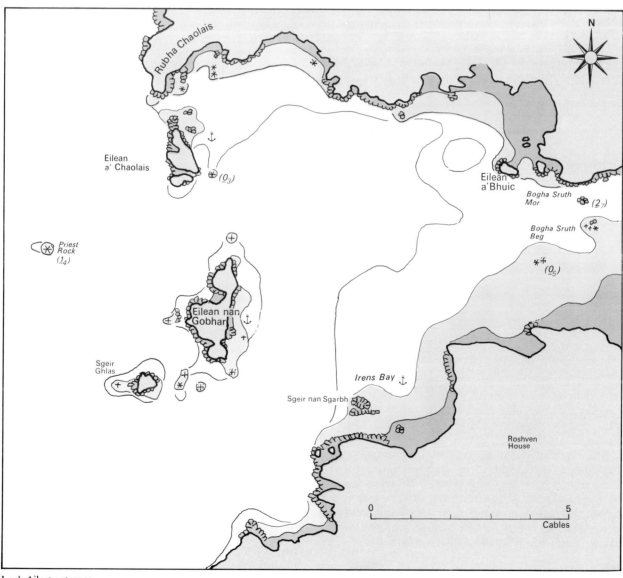

Loch Ailort entrance

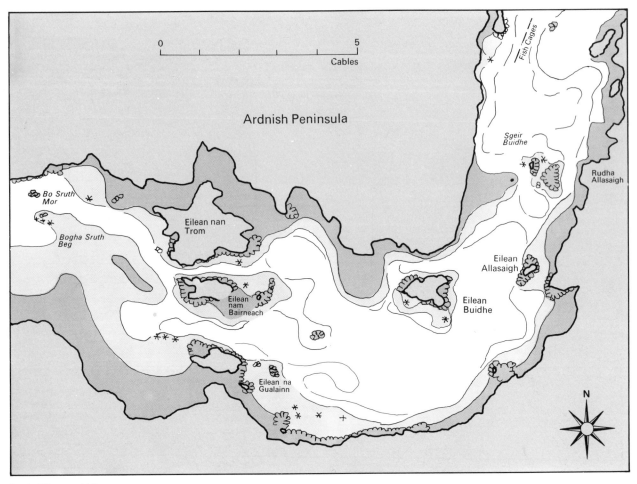

Loch Ailort – middle part

Approach before half-flood so that the Bogha Sruths are visible, and pass between them. If both are covered, there is enough depth to pass north of Bogha Sruth Mor within ¼ cable of the shore.

After passing these rocks head for the southern half of Eilean nan Trom; then bring the east end of Eilean na Gualainn in line with the west end of Eilean nam Bairneach 140°, to pass between a drying rock west of Eilean nan Trom and a drying bank a cable further west.

The channel between Eilean nan Trom and Eilean nam Bairneach may be taken; a line to clear the drying reef a cable east of Eilean nam Bairneach is the north end of Goat Island touching the south point of Eilean nan Trom 272°.

Alternatively pass west of Eilean nam Bairneach, keeping ½ cable off that island, and follow round to pass midway between Eilean nam Bairneach and Eilean na Gualainn.

After the east end of Eilean na Gualainn has been passed, its north point in line with the most northerly point of the south shore, 278°, leads south of Bogha Druim a' Loch. South of that line is a designated area for permanent moorings, and a designated anchorage lies immediately to the east, off the south shore south of Eilean Buidhe.

There are no other regular anchorages here, nor at the head of the loch, but if your taste for rock-dodging hasn't been exhausted, the following will guide you through the upper part of the loch.

Head of Loch Ailort
56°52'N 5°41'W

Keep at least a cable south of Eilean Buidhe to avoid a drying rock, pass about ½ cable northwest of Eilean Allasaigh and steer towards Rudha Allasaigh, 3 cables further NNE.

Pass about ¼ cable off the point of Rudha Allasaigh to avoid a large area of rocks which covers at HW, ½ cable from the shore.

The spit on the west side, west of these rocks, has a boulder at its outer end which covers above half-tide.

If the boulder is visible, an alternative course is to pass about 30 metres east of it, heading NNW.

About 4 cables further north a rock in the middle of the loch dries about 1 metre; it lies midway between two tidal islets, one on either shore. A line of fish cages is moored off the west shore here.

A mile further northeast the Black Islands (Eilean Dubh) lie on the southeast side of the loch. A survey of 1860 shows moderate depths among them, with a bottom of sand as well as some rock.

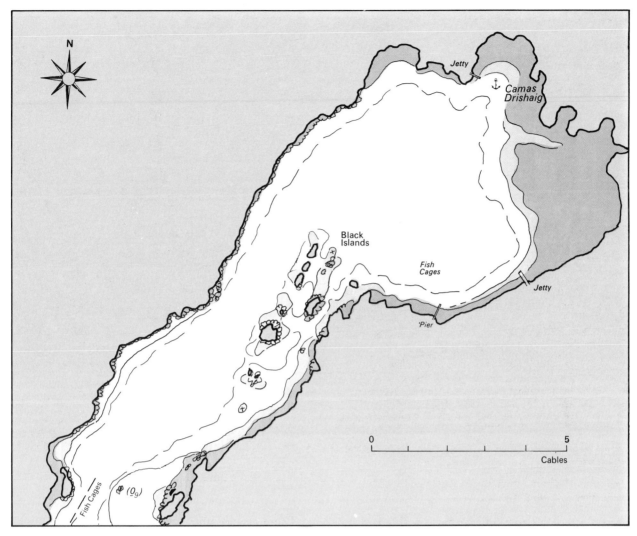

Head of Loch Ailort

Note the submerged rock 1 cable south of the most southerly above-water rock, as well as a drying rock ¼ cable off the east shore.

The head of the loch is a deep basin about ¾ mile across with an extensive fish-farming industry.

The east side of the basin dries for about 3 cables and the most suitable anchorage is at the mouth of Camas Drishaig on the northeast side of the basin.

Loch nan Ceall (Arisaig Harbour)

Waypoint on leading line 2 cables south of Luinga Mhor 56°53'·7N 5°56'W
See colour photos between pages 58 and 59.

One of the most intimidating entrances of any anchorage on the West Coast, although much easier now that the perches are regularly maintained.

As the Admiralty *West Coast of Scotland Pilot* put it in 1934:

'This tortuous channel, being full of rocks, is dangerous to enter, and as the islets in the vicinity are low and inconspicuous they are of no assistance in fixing the position of a vessel.'

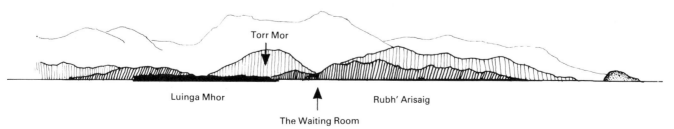

Loch nan Ceall approach from west.

Loch Ailort; the narrows from southwest. *Photo Jean Lawrence.*

Loch nan Ceall and Rubh' Arisaig from southwest.

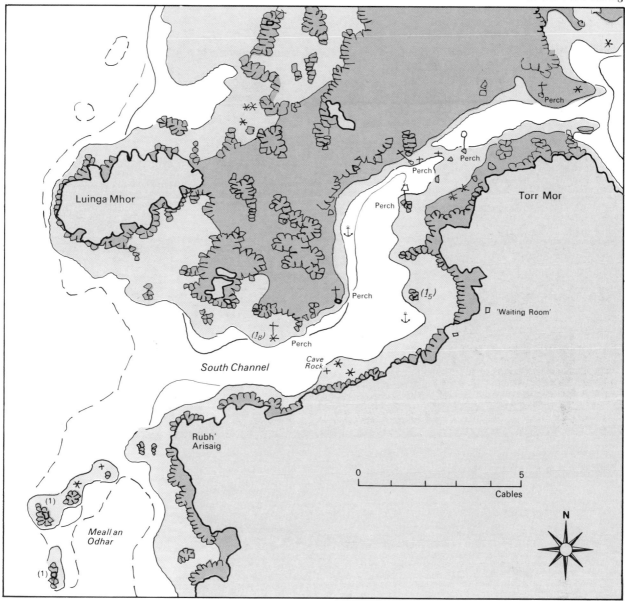

Loch nan Ceall (Arisaig) entrance

The perches, which have been restored by Arisaig Marine, make the entrance channel possible for a stranger – once he has found the entrance.

The perches are difficult to distinguish at HW; you may have to swallow your pride and try to raise Arisaig Marine or a local yachtsman on VHF for advice. It is intended to erect additional perches and, when this is done, the information will be published in a supplement to this guide.

Charts

A photocopy of chart *2817*, published in 1858 (1:10,700) provides the greatest detail, subject to the usual reservations about using obsolete charts (see Appendix I).

Tides

Tidal streams run strongly in the entrance channel, particularly for 1½ hours either side of LW when the banks on either side of the channel are

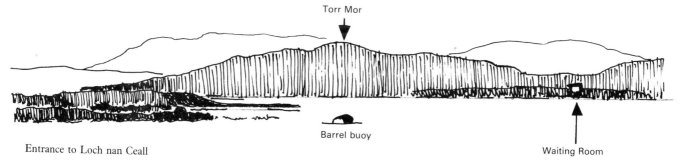

Entrance to Loch nan Ceall

Entrance channel to Loch nan Ceall

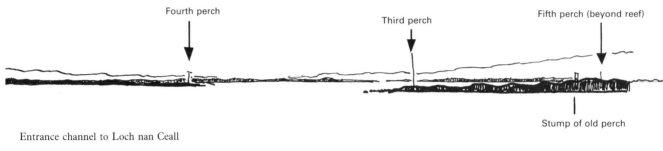

Entrance channel to Loch nan Ceall

Entrance channel to Loch nan Ceall

Loch nan Ceall

uncovered and the flow is concentrated within it. Constant −0040 Ullapool (−0500 Dover).

Height in metres

MHWS	MHWN	MTL	MLWN	MLWS
5·0	3·8	2·9	2·1	0·7

Identification

A bearing 256° astern of the north point of Muck (not Eilean nan Each, which lies northwest of Muck) in line with the southeast point of Eilean Chathastail, southeast of Eigg, leads to the north side of entrance.

In poor visibility note that Luinga Mhor is low and flat.

Rubh' Arisaig stands up rather more than Luinga Mhor and has a patch of white paint on its end, which shows up well from the west.

Dangers and marks in the approach

Meallan Odhar are a group of rocks up to ½ mile WSW of Rubh' Arisaig. The outermost rocks are 1 metre high.

On the north side of the entrance rocks drying up to 3·7 metres extend more than a cable south of the line between Luinga Mhor and the Fraoch Eilean, the islet 3 cables southeast of it.

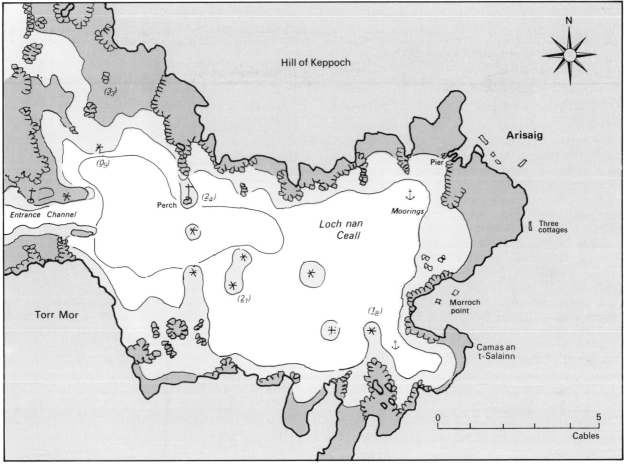

Loch nan Ceall

A rock which dries 1·8 metres, 2 cables southeast of Fraoch Eilean, is marked by an orange perch. Less than half a metre of the perch shows at HWS; take care not to confuse with second perch.

A second (orange) perch lies 2 cables ENE of the first. The rock which it marks covers at HW springs and extends about 20 metres south of the perch.

Cave Rock, lying about a cable off the south shore and nearly 2 cables south of the second perch, dries at LW.

The Waiting Room (so called because it used to provide shelter for passengers waiting for steamers) is an inconspicuous grey cottage ½ mile east of the second perch.

Approach

From south keep at least a cable west of Meallan Odhar and north of Rubh' Arisaig, and pass 1 cable south of the two perches described above.

The Waiting Room, under a prominent dip in the hills immediately behind it, bearing 080°, leads clear between the dangers in the entrance.

From north it is essential to identify Luinga Mhor and pass southwest of it; yachts have in the past mistaken the passage and attempted to enter north of the island, with disastrous results.

Steer southeast towards the north side of Rubh' Arisaig until the perches and the Waiting Room are identified, and pass a cable south of the perches.

Anchorages

Temporary anchorage can be found either ¼ mile west of the Waiting Room or, in better shelter, NNE of the second perch, on the west side of the channel.

The entrance channel

See colour photos between pages 58 and 59.

For most of the next mile the channel is from ½ to 1 cable wide between drying rocks and sandbanks, of which the most prominent are marked by four more perches, two to be left on each hand.

These may be difficult to pick out at HW when little of them is showing, or at LW when they are hidden among the labyrinth of rocks. Owing to the twists of the channel, each perch seems to appear in a surprising place in relation to the previous one. Make quite sure that each perch is the one you think it is.

The third perch, 3½ cables NNE of the second, is a black and white pole with no topmark. If it should collapse (as it has in the past), take care at high tide not to be deceived by the stump of an old perch on the highest point of the reef, which is a long way from the end.

The fourth perch (orange) lies 1 cable NNE of the third, and is left to port; this one is a little over half a metre high at HWS.

25

The fifth perch (fluorescent green), 2 cables east of the fourth, is left to starboard.

Between these two perches the bottom is shallow and rocky with depths of less than 1·5 metres, and the passage should be avoided by boats of deeper draught near LW springs.

The sixth perch (orange), lying ¼ mile ENE of the fifth, is left to port.

For a further 2 cables, drying sandbanks lie on either side of the channel, with a drying rock on the north bank; this north bank extends south of a direct line to the next perch.

Keep a careful check astern at this point to make sure you are not being set off course, especially if you are so rash as to try to enter against the ebb.

When leaving, a useful line for the part of the channel between the second and third perches is the line of a road on the south shore. It has been observed that the first perch is more conspicuous than the second and a visiting yacht was observed setting a direct course from the third perch to the first.

Arisaig Harbour
56°54'·5N 5°51'W
Arisaig village lies at the east side of a basin, about 1½ miles from the sixth perch.

South of the village stands a group of low cottages and, south of them again, several detached houses among trees.

From a point ½ cable south of the sixth perch steer for the three low cottages and keep them bearing 090°.

Another perch (orange) lies ½ mile east of the sixth, on a rock which dries 2·4 metres, 1½ cables from the north shore of the basin.

Pass ¼ cable south of this perch to avoid a rock which dries 0·6 metres, 1 cable south of it, and continue to head for the cottages.

Anchor clear of moorings off the pier in the northeast corner of the basin, and clear of the approach to the pier which is used regularly by the passenger boat *Etive Shearwater*.

The inlet at the pier dries at LW springs; yachts may go alongside on a rising tide if access is not needed for the *Shearwater*. Keep the south face of the pier well open to avoid reefs at the entrance.

Trailed boats may be launched from a slip at the head of the inlet if the slipway is not occupied (ask first).

Camas an t-Salainn in the southeast corner of the basin has several licensed moorings in it with wide swinging circles, but there may be space in which to anchor.

Approach from the north to avoid rocks shown on the plan.

Services and supplies
Moorings, repairs, diesel, *Calor Gas*, water at pier. Slipway with cradle on rails. Shop, hotel, restaurant.

Communications
Post office, phone box, train and bus to Mallaig and Glasgow. Arisaig Marine ☎ Arisaig 01687 450224 or 450678.

North Channel
North of the skerries in the entrance lies the North Channel, of which the current *Admiralty Pilot* drily observes, 'it is seldom used, even by vessels with local knowledge'. It would be impossible to provide pilotage notes; use the old chart if you must try it.

Passage notes
North of Loch nan Ceall, drying rocks extend more than a mile from the shore; in poor visibility keep outwith the 15-metre contour or set a compass course to avoid the risk of following the coastline in among the rocks.

Morar River
56°58'N 5°50'W
See colour photo facing this page

A river estuary 5 miles north of the entrance to Loch nan Ceall with a winding channel, in which the depth is mostly less than half a metre, between inviting banks of white sand, which feature regularly in Tourist Board brochures.

The entrance has a bar, on most of which there is no more than 0·2 metres and the position of the deepest part varies.

The slightest swell would make the entrance hazardous even to a shoal-draught boat except perhaps during the last quarter of the flood.

Several yachts are kept on moorings at the head of the estuary, but there must be many occasions when the sea on the bar makes it impossible to go out.

A keelboat might find a place to lie afloat at the most northerly point of the channel at neaps, but it could only to be considered by owners of twin-keel and shoal-draught yachts.

The colour photo facing this page should be studied closely as there is no detailed survey. A sand spit usually extends northwest from the south point of the entrance and a successful approach is only likely to be made from that direction. Make for the south point of the entrance and then follow the channel by eye in the clear water.

Supplies
Shop, hotel, garage, post office, phone box.

Conditions off Ardnamurchan can be lumpy
Photo: Rinze van der Bij

Morar Estuary from west. The spit outside the bar can be seen, lower right (see facing page)

Castle Tioram in Loch Moidart (see page 15)

Moidart North Channel from northwest, about half tide (see page 16)

Morar River from south with the head of the estuary at bottom right

Mallaig

Waypoint ½ cable north of light buoy north of Sgeir Dhearg 57°00'·8N 5°49'·5W

This busy fishing harbour and ferry terminal lies at the south point of the entrance to Loch Nevis, 7½ miles north of Loch nan Ceall. Its main attraction is the wide range of services available, but yachts have to take their chance among working boats. At present, yachts are recommended to visit Mallaig only during daytime.

Mallaig Harbour is currently being extended by building a new basin on the north side and when this is complete (summer 1998) more space should be available in the inner harbour.

Glaschoille, on the north side of Loch Nevis, 4 miles from Mallaig, may be found more peaceful in northerly winds.

Charts

2208 (1:50,000); plan (1:7,500) on chart *2534*

Tides

The constant is −0050 Ullapool (−0500 Dover)

Height in metres

MHWS	MHWN	MTL	MLWN	MLWS
5·0	3·8	2·9	2·1	0·7

Approach

If possible, call up the harbourmaster before entering for advice on where to berth.

From south and west Eilean na h-Acairseid and large industrial buildings on Rubha na h-Acairseid, ENE of the island, help to identify the entrance in poor visibility.

The passage south of Sgeir Dhearg may be obstructed by works for the new harbour basin.

Identify the stbd-hand light buoy NNE of Sgeir Dhearg and approach on a heading not less than 030° to clear the north end of Sgeir Dhearg and pass north of the buoy.

From north pass between Sgeir Dhearg and the mainland.

A G con light buoy has been laid northeast of Sgeir Dearg.

Mallaig. An extension to the harbour is being built between the Steamer Pier in the middle of the photograph and Sgeir Dearg at the left-hand side

Traffic signals three vertical red lights at the head of the Steamer Pier indicate that a large vessel is entering or leaving the harbour, and small craft should keep clear of the entrance.

Lights

At night, the lights may be difficult to identify against the lights of the town.

Sgeir Dhearg Fl(2)WG.8s6m5M
Steamer Pier extension Iso.WRG.4s6m9-6M, with a separate light Fl.G.3s14m6M

From south or west approach in the white sector of Sgeir Dhearg light. Identify the light buoy NNE of Sgeir Dhearg and steer to keep it bearing not less than 030°, leave the buoy to stbd and steer for the light at Steamer Pier.

From north pass into the green sector of Sgeir Dhearg light and into the white sector of the Steamer Pier light.

Anchorage

Anchor in the southeast corner of the harbour or as directed by the harbourmaster. There are many moorings and the bottom is foul.

Supplies and services

Boatyard, engineer, diesel, petrol, *Calor Gas*, water at pier.

Chandler and chart agent. Shops, including chemist and butcher, bank, hotels.

Communications

Train and bus to Glasgow, ferry to Skye, post office, phone box. Harbourmaster ☎ 01687 2154. Boatyard (Henderson) ☎ 01687 2304. Chandler and chart agent (Johnston Bros) ☎ 01687 2215.

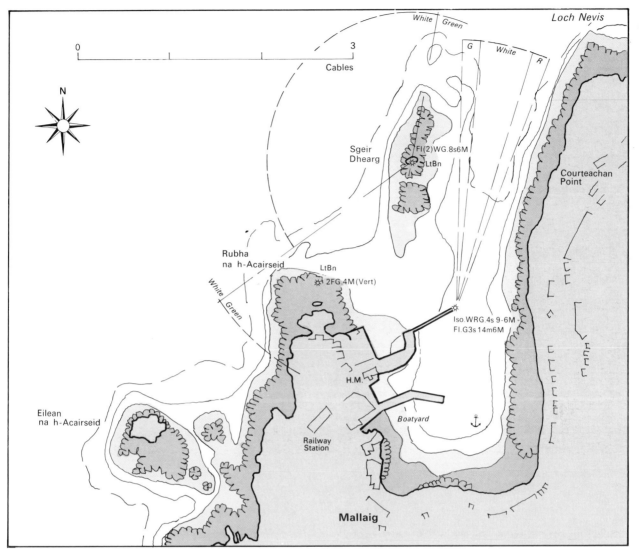

0   3

Cables

N

Loch Nevis

White | Green

G | White | R

Sgeir
Dhearg

Fl(2)WG.8s6M

LtBn

Courteachan
Point

Rubha
na h-Acairseid

LtBn

2FG.4M(Vert)

White | Green

Iso.WRG.4s 9·6M
Fl.G3s 14m6M

Eilean
na h-Acairseid

H.M.

Boatyard

Railway
Station

Mallaig

Mallaig harbour

II. The Small Isles

This is the group of four islands between Ardnamurchan and Skye, each inhabited by a small community and each of very different character.

Only Canna, the most northwesterly of the Small Isles, has a good sheltered anchorage and it makes an ideal staging post on the way to the Outer Hebrides.

The Small Isles and Ardnamurchan looking N

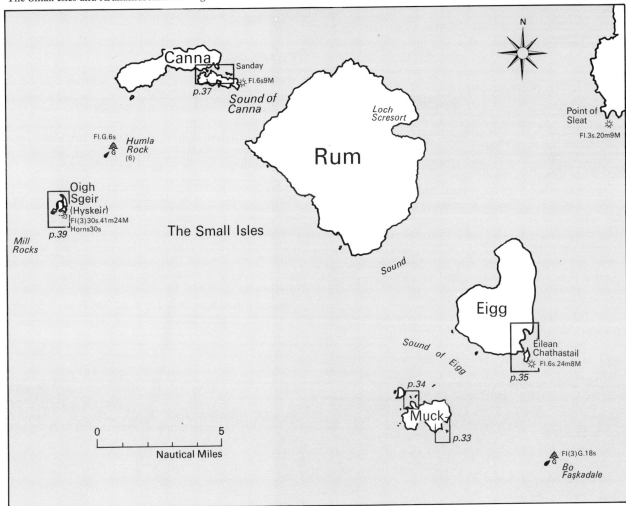

Charts

The only charts showing the Small Isles in any detail are *2207* and *2208* at 1:50,000. Even these don't include the whole of Canna; chart *1795* does so, but only at 1:100,000. Ordnance Survey map *39* neatly covers all the Small Isles at 1:50,000.

Tides

On the west side of Eigg the constant averages −0048 Ullapool (−0508 Dover).

Height in metres

MHWS	MHWN	MTL	MLWN	MLWS
4·7	3·5	2·6	1·6	0·5

Among the Small Isles the flood stream runs generally northwestwards and northwards, and both flood and ebb reach a rate of 4 knots in places, particularly east of Eigg, between Muck and Eigg, and around the rocks between Canna and Hyskeir.

Heavy overfalls occur wherever there are relatively shallow banks.

Steep seas are reflected off the west point of Rum in strong westerly winds.

Among the Small Isles the streams turn approximately as follows:

The north-going stream begins +0600 Ullapool (+0140 Dover)

The south-going stream begins HW Ullapool (−0420 Dover).

Dangers

Many drying rocks extend up to ¼ mile off the shores of the Small Isles so that the chart must be carefully studied before approaching the shore. (A rock north of Rum was only reported in 1991 and may not be on your chart.)

Banks and rocks east and southeast of Eigg and Muck are described in the previous chapter.

In the passage between Muck and Eigg, 6 cables north of Muck, Godag is a group of rocks of which the most southerly is above water, with drying and submerged rocks up to 3 cables further north.

Southwest of Canna there are several rocks between Canna and Hyskeir (Oigh Sgeir) and there is some doubt as to the completeness of the survey here.

Marks

The best identification is the shape of the islands themselves. Rum is high and mountainous; Eigg has the long ridge of the Sgurr lying on an east-west axis at its south end which from the east looks like a rock pinnacle.

Good use can be made of transits of the edges of any two islands, and this is particularly valuable as there are several magnetic anomalies in the area.

Lights

Ardnamurchan lighthouse Fl.20s55m24M
Eigg (SE point of Eilean Chathastail) Fl.6s24m8M
Canna (E end of Sanday) Fl.6s32m9M
Hyskeir (Oigh Sgeir) Fl(3)30s41m24M
Bo Faskadale buoy 6M NE of Ardnamurchan Fl(3)G.18s

Isle of Muck

Muck is the least visited of the Small Isles, partly because of the incomplete shelter of its anchorages.

However it is a most attractive place in an undramatic way and, short of a failure of the weather forecasts, one anchorage or the other should provide good shelter.

The island has been run successfully as an agricultural estate by the McEwen family for very many years.

Port Mor

Waypoint on leading line 329° southeast of Sgeir Dubh 56°49'·2N 6°12'·7W
See colour photo between pages 58 and 59

At the southeast side of the island, Port Mor is the main harbour, but the rocks at the entrance do not completely protect it from any sea from south.

Dubh Sgeir, an above-water rock, lies in the middle of the entrance, with drying reefs joining it to the west point of the inlet and extending ½ cable all round.

Bogha Ruadh a detached drying reef, lies about a cable to the east of Dubh Sgeir, south of a drying reef extending ¼ mile south of the east point of the inlet.

A shoal patch with a depth of less than 2 metres lies in the passage between these two rocks.

Muck. Port Mor approach

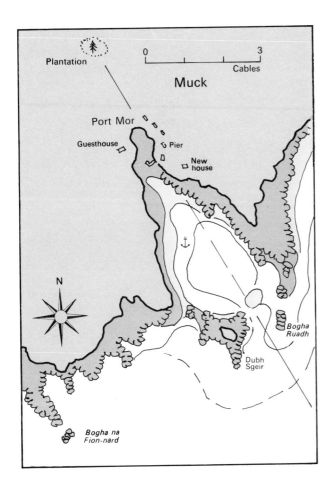

Gallanach (Bagh a' Ghallanaich)

Waypoint ¼ mile north of Bohaund 56°51'·1N 6°15'·5W
See colour photo between pages 58 and 59.

The entrance to this bay on the north side of Muck is obstructed by drying reefs, but these only offer limited protection from seas from the north.

Tides

Tides run at 4 knots at springs in the Sound of Eigg, between Eigg and Muck, as well as on the west side of Muck, but less strongly across the mouth of the bay itself.

Dangers and marks

Horse Island (Eilean nan Each) is attached to the northwest point of Muck by drying reefs.

Godag, a detached rock 6 cables north of Muck, about a mile east of Horse Island, has drying and submerged rocks ¼ mile north of it.

Drying reefs extend several cables northwest from the east point of the bay.

Bohaund, a detached reef which dries 1·2 metres, lies in the middle of the entrance.

Approach

From east pass south of Godag, and head for the north end of Horse Island.

The gap between Lamb Island (Eilean Ard nan Uan) and Lamb Point, immediately south of it, appears as a square notch in the skyline. When this closes, head for the south end of Lamb Island,

The leading line is the gable end of the left-hand and lower of two cottages at the pier under the middle of a group of trees on the hillside beyond the head of the inlet bearing 329°.

Other houses could be mistaken for the cottage at the pier, which is hidden from a yacht coming from the east until almost on the line.

Approach

The leading line is not easy to make out but must be positively identified before entering.

From east or northeast, keep the east shore of Muck open of the west shore of Eigg, bearing 360° astern, until the leading line is identified, to clear Bogha Ruadh.

Anchorage

Clear of moorings and drying reefs on the northeast side of the inlet.

Small shoal-draught boats may find space to dry out in complete shelter behind the L-shaped stone jetty at the head of the inlet.

A new jetty, which also dries, has been built on the northeast side of the inlet.

No supplies. Phone box near the pier. The new guesthouse can provide meals if arranged in advance.

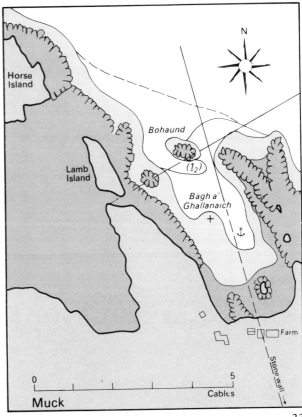

Gallanach Bay, Isle of Muck. The leading line to clear the east side of Bohaund is the middle of the doors in the gable end of the barn with the round roof in line with the edge of the wall on the shoulder of the hill beyond

keeping the gap well closed, to clear the reef on the east side of Gallanach Bay.

A line which leads between Bohaund and the reef to the east, consists of a pale yellow barn with a curved roof at the west side of the farm under the highest point of a stone wall on the left shoulder of the hill beyond; a newer barn (which is not the one you want) has been built close west of the first one.

About 2 cables south of Bohaund lies a rock awash. Anchor north or northwest of the tidal islet towards the head of the bay.

A roll-on ferry terminal is planned, details of which, when built, will be included in a supplement.

Isle of Eigg

Waypoint ¼ mile southwest of Eilean Chaisteal 56°52'N 6°08'W

Eigg is the most easterly of the Small Isles and is large enough to have a substantial population, most of whom live at the northwest side of the island.

The main anchorage (56°53'N 6°08'W) lies at the southeast side, in the channel between Eigg and Eilean Castle (Eilean Chathastail), but the shelter is not very good, except for shoal-draught boats which may be able to use a drying boat harbour NNW of the pier.

Tides

Constant averages +0132 Ullapool (−0508 Dover)

Height in metres

MHWS	MHWN	MTL	MLWN	MLWS
4·7	3·5	2·6	1·6	0·5

The tide runs strongly through the anchorage, the flood running northwards, turning south 2 hours before HW.

Off the east side of Eigg streams run at 4 knots at springs, causing a heavy sea with wind against tide, and making approach from the east difficult.

Dangers and marks

Eilean Castle is 35 metres high, grass-covered, with a white light beacon on its southeast side.

Drying rocks extend a cable south and southwest of Eilean Castle.

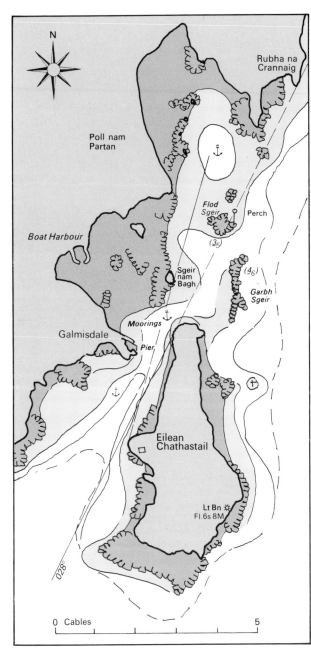

Galmisdale

Sgeir nam Bagh stands above water on the east side of a drying reef, less than a cable NNW of Eilean Castle.

Between Eilean Castle and Rubha na Crammaig, half a mile north, lie a group of drying reefs, with a reasonably clear passage between them.

Garbh Sgeir on the southeast side of the passage dries 4·7 metres, marked by a rather temporary-seeming can buoy. There are plans to restore the former beacon on Garbh Sgeir – this will be noted in a future supplement.

Flod Sgeir on the northwest side, which dries 3·5 metres, is marked by a perch with a ring topmark.

Approach

From south keep 2 cables off the southwest point of Eilean Castle to avoid the drying reefs there. Rubha na Crannaig, the east point of Eigg, open west of the north point of Eilean Castle 028° leads clear of these reefs.

From east identify the perch on Flod Sgeir and pass ¼ cable southeast of it heading southwest for Sgeir nam Bagh, then south towards Galmisdale Point.

Anchorages

South of Galmisdale Point clear of reefs which dry 1 cable from northwest side, and also clear of the strong tide in the narrows.

North end of Eilean Castle. There is not usually space to anchor near the jetty owing to the moorings, and there is a risk of fouling ground tackle.

Shoal-draught boats may be able to anchor inshore of the moorings, or dry out in the boat harbour at the head of the bay near HW.

Anchor as convenient between Eilean Castle and Sgeir nam Bagh, avoiding the reef drying SSW from Sgeir nam Bagh, and also avoiding obstructing the passage which is used by various ferries.

A roll-on ferry terminal is planned, full details of which will be included in a future supplement.

poles in line 110°

Eigg leading line

Eigg – Flod Sgeir at low tide.

Eigg – anchorages from the north shore of Poll nam Partan. The arrow shows the line to take to Poll nam Partan.

Galmisdale approach from northeast

Poll nam Partan, ½ mile north of Eilean Castle, has a depth of 2·5 metres at the deepest part, but no more than 0·5 metre in the approach.

Enter the pool at a suitable rise of tide between Flod Sgeir and Eigg, keeping the east side of Sgeir nam Bagh in line with the west side of Eilean Castle.

Anchor on sand clear of rock or weed, easily visible in the clear water, wherever depth and swinging room can be found.

All of these anchorages are only safe in moderate weather.

Supplies and services

Diesel, water, *Calor Gas*, coffee shop at jetty; phone box on its northwest side. Post office and shop 2 miles along road to Laig. Ferries to Mallaig, Arisaig and Glenuig. Estate office ☎ Mallaig 0687 82428.

Laig Bay on the northwest side of Eigg provides occasional anchorage in offshore winds. The bay is notable for its 'singing sands' in certain conditions. Two light-coloured poles in line near the south end of the bay bearing 110° lead close in to clear water over a sandy bottom clear of offlying rocks in the north part of the bay (see photo).

Isle of Rum

The largest of the Small Isles, Rum is spectacularly mountainous. It is owned by Scottish Natural Heritage, and used for research into the breeding of red deer, with a sideline in white-tailed sea eagles. Access may be restricted to two marked trails from Loch Scresort, on the east side of the island.

Landing is only permitted at Loch Scresort, and dogs may not be taken ashore.

Access to some areas of the island may be restricted.

Kinloch Castle, built in 1903, has been used as an hotel but is currently closed.

Dangers

Off the north point of Rum several drying rocks lie up to ¼ mile from the land (one of which was only reported in 1991 and may not be on your chart); these are avoided by keeping outwith the 15-metre contour.

At the west point of Rum drying reefs extend 1 cable from the shore, and any sea from the west is reflected and becomes particularly steep and confused.

Loch Scresort

Waypoint mid entrance to Loch Scresort 57°01'N 6°14'·5W

An inlet more than a mile long on the east side of Rum, shoaling very gradually towards the head, subject to violent squalls in strong westerly winds, and swell with easterly winds.

Drying reefs extend nearly ¼ mile from the south shore at the entrance, and there are drying rocks close inshore on the north side.

The bottom is sand with patches of weed.

A roll-on ferry terminal is planned, full details of which will be included in a future supplement.

Approach

Keep well off the south shore on entering, and anchor off the concrete slip on the south side of the loch, or northeast of the stone pier further in.

Supplies

Basic stores at shop. Phone box and post office.

Isle of Canna

Canna is the most westerly of the Small Isles with a well-sheltered natural harbour, often used by yachts on passage to the Outer Hebrides, as well as by fishing boats. Its climate is better than its neighbours', having no mountains to the west, and it has white sandy beaches.

Canna has been presented to the National Trust for Scotland by John Lorne Campbell, its owner for many years.

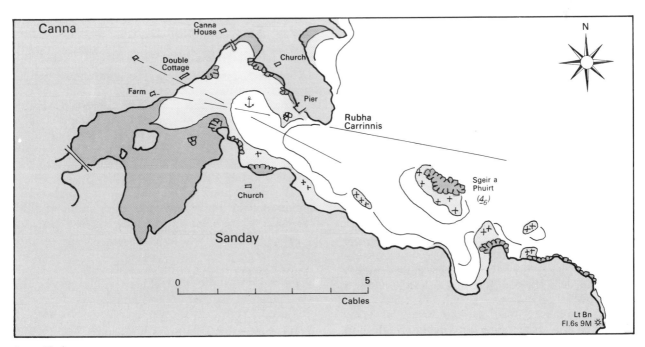

Canna Harbour

Canna Harbour

Waypoint northeast of Sgeir a' Phuirt 57°03'·4N 6°28'·7W
See colour photo facing page 59.

Dangers and marks

Rocks off the north coast of Rum referred to above must be avoided by keeping at least ½ mile off shore.

The north side of Canna is clean beyond a cable from the shore.

Between the south side of Canna and Hyskeir there are several rocks for which chart *1795* must be consulted (see also Hyskeir, below).

The east point of Sanday on the south side of Canna Harbour is marked by a small but conspicuous white light beacon.

Sgeir a' Phuirt, an extensive reef between the light beacon and the harbour entrance, dries 4·6 metres, 2 cables north of Sanday.

Inside the harbour on the southwest side of Rubha Carrinnis, the north point of the entrance, is a new concrete pier. A roll-on ferry terminal is planned, details of which will be included in a future supplement.

West of the pier lies a drying rock, with a shoal spit southwest of it.

The harbour shoals gradually towards the northwest shore, with a clean sandy bottom.

Compass Hill at the northeast point of Canna causes abnormal magnetic variation to the east of Canna.

Approach

Identify the farm towards the west end of the harbour and keep it in line with the south side of Rubha Carrinnis to lead north of Sgeir a' Phuirt.

Keep to the south half of the entrance to avoid the rock west of the pier. This rock can be avoided by keeping a conspicuous cottage on the hillside open southwest of the southwest end of a pair of cottages on the shore.

Lights

Sanday light beacon Fl.6s32m9M is obscured between 061° and 152°. There are no lights to lead into the harbour.

Anchorage

Anchor wherever there is enough depth; a good guide is to bring a prominent white stone cross in the churchyard on the northeast side of the harbour under the summit of Compass Hill.

Fishing boats used to congregate in Canna Harbour during the hours of darkness, but there are now few of them. Nevertheless, show a good anchor light and, if you use a tripping line, secure it inboard.

There is enough weed on the bottom for new arrivals to provide plenty of entertainment for those already securely anchored.

Land below the church on the northeast side; the stone jetty in front of Canna House is private.

No supplies. Phone box and post office at the pair of cottages on the northwest side of the harbour.

Canna Boat Harbour

The bay between the west end of Sanday and the south side of Canna provides a temporary anchorage in very quiet weather.

There are many rocks in the approach and Sgeirean Dubha, 2 metres high, in the middle of the entrance, is the key to the approach.

A rock which just dries, 4 cables southwest of the entrance, is cleared by keeping Sgeirean Dubha in line with the summit of Compass Hill bearing 051°.

Pass between Sgeirean Dubha and the rock northwest of it which covers at HW.

Tarbert Bay (57°03'N 6°32'W) lies a mile west of Sanday, southeast of a dip in the skyline of Canna.

Identify Haslam, an islet 3 cables off Canna, rather closer to the west side of the bay than to Sanday.

Keep at least ¼ mile off Haslam and approach the bay, keeping closer to its west side than to Haslam.

Anchor towards the northeast side of the bay, clear of rocks.

Hyskeir (Oigh Sgeir)

56°58'N 6°41'W
See colour photo facing page 59.

A group of low islets 5 miles southwest of Canna with a white lighthouse 39 metres high.

It is only rarely visited by yachts and is not recommended as there is almost no shelter. The lighthouse is to be 'de-manned' in 1997.

Dangers and marks

Humla Rock, 5 metres high, lying between Hyskeir and Canna, has a green conical light buoy (Fl.G.6s) on its southwest side.

Submerged rocks and shoals lie around Humla, and between that rock and Canna.

The usual passage from Ardnamurchan to the Minch lies between Hyskeir and the Humla buoy.

Mill Rocks, 2¼ miles southwest of Hyskeir, have depths of less than 2 metres. For a further 3 miles southwest seas break in strong winds owing to the uneven bottom.

The north point of Eigg just open of the south point of Rum 085° leads 1½ miles south of Mill Rocks.

A white lighthouse 39 metres in height stands on Hyskeir.

Approach and anchorage

To anchor at Hyskeir the following course has been followed: pass 1 cable west of the north end of Hyskeir and steer 170° to keep open the narrow channel between Hyskeir and Garbh Sgeir on its

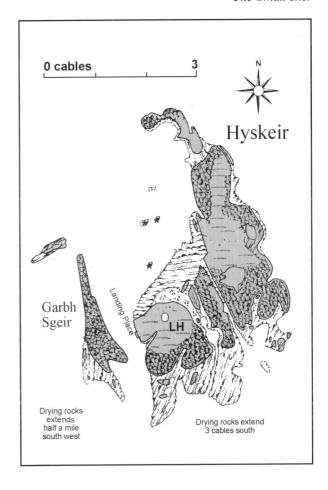

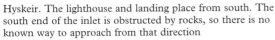
Hyskeir. The lighthouse and landing place from south. The south end of the inlet is obstructed by rocks, so there is no known way to approach from that direction

west side, to avoid a drying rock in the bay northwest of the lighthouse.

Although this course has been taken successfully in the past, it should certainly not be assumed that there are no other rocks around.

The landing place is on the east side of the channel between Hyskeir and Garbh Sgeir, and there are three mooring rings on Garbh Sgeir opposite the landing place. The bottom is sand, with a depth of about 3 metres.

Many rocks lie off the south end of the channel, so that an approach from that direction should not be attempted.

III. West coast of Skye

Passage notes – Point of Sleat to Soay

Charts
2208 (1:50,000)

OS map *32*

OS Outdoor Leisure Map – The Cuillin and Torridon Hills (1:25,000)

Tides

The north-going stream begins about +0535 Ullapool (+0115 Dover)

The south-going stream begins about −0025 Ullapool (−0445 Dover)

On the west side of Point of Sleat there is probably an eddy with the north-going stream, and overfalls occur west and southwest of the point with both flood and ebb tides.

Dangers and marks

Point of Sleat is low and rocky with a 7-metre white light beacon at its southwest tip.

Rocks, above water and drying, extend 1¾ cables west of the point to Sgeir Dhubh which is 0·3 metre high.

Lights

Point of Sleat Fl.3s20m9M

Sanday (southeast of Canna) Fl.6s32m9M

Mallaig (see Chapter I)

Shelter

Moderate shelter may be found in Loch Slapin, Loch Eishort (difficult approach), and Soay Harbour (which has a tidal sill). Canna (see Chapter II) provides some of the best shelter in the area. If heavy westerly weather is expected, consider Sound of Sleat (see Chapter IV), Mallaig or Arisaig (Chapter I).

Occasional anchorages

Tarskavaig (57°07'N 6°00'W), and Ob Gauscavaig (Tokavaig), a mile northwest of Tarskavaig, provide occasional anchorages in settled weather.

Supplies

Nearest (limited) at Rum; otherwise Malaig, Arisaig (Chapter I), or Loch Harport below.

Heading for the hills: the Cuillins, Skye

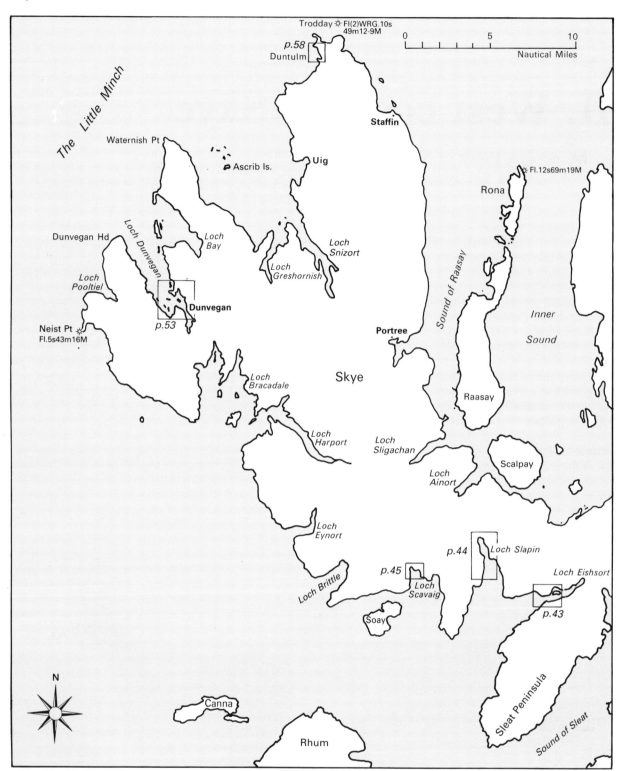

Loch Eishort

57°10'N 5°55'W

Tides

Constant −0040 Ullapool (−0500 Dover)

Height in metres

MHWS	MHWN	MTL	MLWN	MLWS
4·8	3·7	2·8	2·1	0·7

Dangers and marks

Drying reefs extend more than a cable southwest of Rubha Suishnish, the north point of the entrance.

Two miles further east the loch narrows abruptly with islets and drying rocks up to ½ mile off Rubha Dubh Ard at the south side.

Sgeir an t-Sruith, about 4 cables north of Dubh Ard, stands above water with drying reefs extending from it to the north shore.

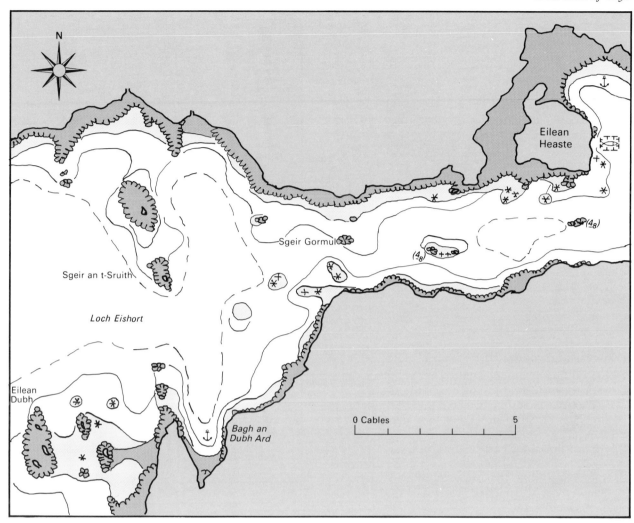

Loch Eishort

Loch Eishort from south of Sgeir an t-Sruith.

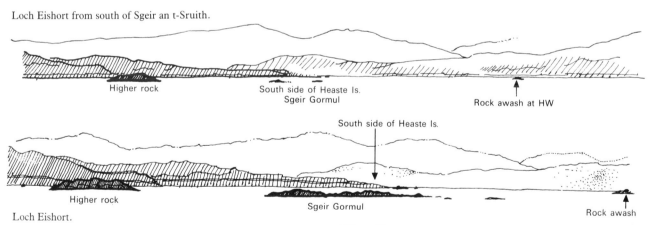

Loch Eishort.

A drying reef extends about ¼ cable south of Sgeir an t-Sruith and drying reefs also lie up to 2 cables north of Dubh Ard, leaving a passage ¼ mile wide.

Many rocks which cover lie in the next 1½ miles but one, which lies north of Sgeir Gormul on the chart, rarely if ever covers.

There appears to be a discrepancy on chart *2208*: Sgeir Gormul itself covers at half tide and is not, as shown on the chart, above water.

Directions

Because of this apparent discrepancy, particular care is necessary, but I have made my way into and out of Loch Eishort as follows.

Pass 1 cable south of Sgeir an t-Sruith, identify the rock north of Sgeir Gormul and pass within ¼ cable of its south side.

If Sgeir Gormul is showing the passage between this and the rock north of it is straightforward.

Pass either side of the group of rocks 3 cables further east and south of the most southerly rock south of Heast Island.

43

Continue east for ¼ mile before turning north and anchor north of the fish cages in the bay east of the island.

Anchorage

Bagh an Dubh Ard, on the south side of the narrows, is an occasional anchorage; when approaching from the west keep closer to Sgeir an t-Sruith than to Dubh Ard to avoid reefs off Dubh Ard; the bottom shelves steeply.

Loch Slapin

57°12'N 6°01'W

Tides

Constant -0040 Ullapool (-0500 Dover)

Height in metres

MHWS	MHWN	MTL	MLWN	MLWS
4·8	3·7	2·8	2·1	0·7

Dangers and marks

Fierce gusts can be expected from the hills at the head of the loch and blowing out of the entrance.

Bogha Ailean lies ¼ mile off the west shore 2 miles NNE of Strathaird Point at a depth of 1·8 metres; The southeast point of Rum open of Strathaird Point, 212°, clears this rock.

Drying reefs extend more than a cable southwest of Rubha Suishnish, the east point of the entrance.

Sharp blocks, drying and just submerged, lie off Rubha Cruaidhlinn.

Rocks drying and awash lying south and west of Sgeir Mhor on the east side of the loch are cleared by keeping a white heap of quarry waste just open west of Dun Mhor, a prominent knob on the east side of the loch (but note that another pile of quarry waste further east is more conspicuous). It would be prudent at low water to keep east of this line while passing Rubha Cruaidhlinn.

Anchorage

The head of the loch dries off for ½ mile and the best anchorage lies on the west side close to the south shore of Bagh nam Faoilean which is steep-to, or north of the fish cages there.

Services

Post office, telephone at Torrin. Water tap at Faoilean.

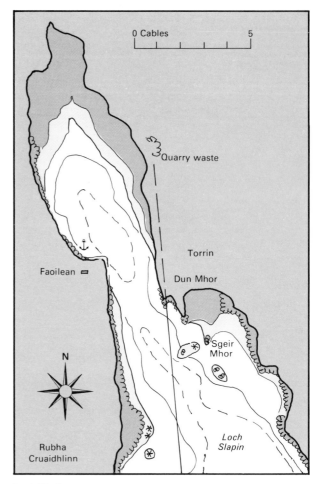

Loch Slapin

Loch Scavaig

Waypoint in fairway east of Eilean Reamhar
57°11'·4N 6°09'·5W

This anchorage can claim to be the most spectacular on the West Coast, surrounded by the jagged peaks of the Cuillin Hills; however the squalls there tend to be equally spectacular.

The 4th edition of the *Admiralty Pilot*, dated 1894 described the Loch in the following words:

'Gairsbheinn, the southern mountain of the south-western ridge, overlooks loch Scathvaig and Soa island. It assumes a remarkable and picturesque appearance; the summit, 2,902 feet high, is like the edge of a knife anil so narrow as scarcely to leave room for the erection of a pile of stones. The south-eastern face forms an arc of a circle to the water's edge, nearly as perfect as could be drawn, with three distinct cliffs separated by steep sloping ledges, round which the sheep walk and are frequently blown over by the rushing gusts of wind, and killed. During a heavy

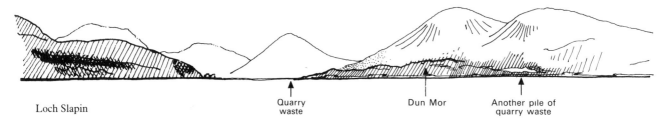

Loch Slapin

fall of rain, the southern and south-western sides of this mountain which, though smooth, are exceedingly steep, present a most singular appearance; the dark heavy cloud round its summit is strongly contrasted by a thousand rills and torrents which pour down its sides and form a perfect network, whilst the two swollen burns at its foot, fall over the cliff in broad and roaring waterfalls. Few more singular and awful sights can be witnessed than the view from the anchorage under Soa, when, during the pauses of a heavy SW gale, the wind and rain suddenly cease, the lower atmosphere clears and discloses the scene described.

In northerly winds, which come on very unexpectedly, the gusts descend the steep sides of Gairsbheinn in sudden and most violent squalls, driving a cloud of foam, like a water spout, before them with a roar like thunder and almost before it has time to drive a vessel at anchor to the extent of her chain, the gust has passed, and for a few moments it is quite calm.'

Tides

Constant −0040 Ullapool (−0500 Dover)

Height in metres

MHWS	MHWN	MTL	MLWN	MLWS
4·8	3·7	2·8	2·1	0·7

Dangers

Drying rocks lie in the middle of the loch leaving a passage 1¼ cables wide east of Eilean Reamhar which lies on the west side of the loch; drying rocks also lie ¼ cable northeast of Eilean Reamhar.

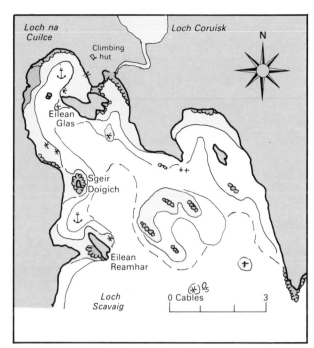

Loch Scavaig

Sgeir Doigich 1½ cables north of Eilean Reamhar occasionally covers, and drying rocks lie off the west shore a cable further northwest.

Loch na Cuilce, Loch Scavaig

Loch Scavaig entrance. The anchorage is behind a low rocky islet in line with the yacht's mast and to the left of the white cottage. Go round the left-hand end of the islet!

Loch na Cuilce

A shallow pool at the head of Loch Scavaig behind Eilean Glas; the entrance to the pool by the west end of Eilean Glas is ¾ cable wide, but a broad drying rock lies 55 metres west of the island. Another small drying rock lies about 10 metres north of the west end of Eilean Glas, and a submerged rock lies close southwest of the island.

Approach

Identify Eilean Reamhar and pass ½ cable east of it as well as Sgeir Doigich.

Pass 20 metres west of Eilean Glas; if the rock west of Eilean Glas is visible it may be passed on its west side although there is less depth there.

It is particularly important to leave swinging room clear of other boats already anchored, as squalls may drive a boat in any direction round her anchor. There are some mooring rings ashore, but their use may be more of a hindrance than help.

An alternative anchorage lies west of the north end of Eilean Reamhar.

Landing steps at the northeast side of Loch na Cuilce are used by tourist boats from Elgol, and dinghies should be left clear of the steps.

Soay Sound

57°10'N 6°14'W

Tides

The tidal stream sets permanently to westward. Confused sea is set up at the west end of the sound with south or southwest winds.

Constant −0040 Ullapool (−0500 Dover)

Height in metres

MHWS	MHWN	MTL	MLWN	MLWS
4·8	3·7	2·8	2·1	0·7

Soay Harbour

See colour photo facing page 90.

The inlet on the north side of Soay is less than a cable wide

A shingle bar across the entrance dries 0·6 metres in the channel, which lies slightly northeast of the middle of the entrance.

Reefs extend ½ cable from the south shore and more than a cable northwest from the northeast point of the entrance.

Approach

Not before half flood, heading southeast towards the buildings and jetty on the northeast shore to avoid drying reefs on the east side; two white poles on the southwest shore in line lead through the deepest part of the channel at the bar.

Soay Harbour entrance from west.

Dangers and marks

A rock which dries 0·6 metre lies less than ½ cable south of the jetty and a drying reef extends towards this rock from the southwest shore, but a narrow passage past the head of the reef leads to an inner pool.

Small buoys on either side of the inlet mark lobster storage creels and you should keep well clear of them when anchoring.

Services

Telephone beside path to cottages at Camas nan Gall.

Other anchorages

An Dubh Chamas, ¾ mile east of Soay Harbour, is well sheltered from southerly winds but may be obstructed by a fish farm.

Camas nan Gall, on the south side of Soay, has poor holding on shingle.

Southwest Coast of Skye from Soay to Neist Point

Waypoint 1 mile WSW of Neist Point 57°25'N 6°24'·5W

The shore of this part of Skye consists of cliffs rising to 285 metres with occasional inlets, of which only Loch Bracadale and Loch Harport offer any shelter.

Charts

1795 (1:100,000) (Loch Eynort is on chart *2208)*
OS maps *23, 32*

Tides

Tidal streams between Soay and Loch Bracadale run at up to 1 knot

The northwest-going stream begins +0535 Ullapool (+0115 Dover)

The southeast-going stream begins −0025 Ullapool (−0445 Dover)

Off Neist Point the northwest-going stream begins −0405 Ullapool (+0400 Dover)

The southeast-going stream begins +0220 Ullapool (−0200 Dover)

From +0535 to −0405 Ullapool (+0115 to −0400 Dover) the south-going stream meets a northwest-going stream and is deflected to the west. Thus, effectively, the stream is running northwest or west for nine hours out of twelve.

Dangers and marks

A magnetic anomaly, which is strongest near the northeast point of Canna, affects all of the area between Loch Brittle and Idrigill Point.

An Dubh Sgeir, 5 metres high, 1½ miles from the shore and 3¼ miles west of Idrigill Point at the west side of Loch Bracadale, is the outermost of a line of rocks known collectively as the Mibow Rocks (Mibogha).

Idrigill Point and Macleod's Maidens from west.

A passage ¼ mile wide lies between Mi-bogha Beag and Mi-bogha Mor.

Macleod's Maidens are a prominent group of rock stacks close to the shore southwest of Idrigill Point.

To pass between Mibow Rocks keep Macleod's Maidens bearing 112°.

Lights

Neist Point Fl.5s43m16M
Sanday (southeast of Canna) Fl.6s32m9M
Oigh Sgeir (Hyskeir) Fl(3)30s41m24M
Ardtreck Point light beacon, Loch Harport
   Iso.4s17m9M

At night

Keep Neist Point bearing more than 330° to clear An Dubh Sgeir.

Shelter

Loch Harport or Canna Harbour.

Minor anchorages

Loch Brittle (57°11'N 6°19'W) A very occasional anchorage, only if there is no swell; shop at camp site.

Loch Eynort (57°14'N 6°22'W) occasional anchorage, if no sea from west. Subject to severe squalls from north.

An Dubh Sgeir, 5 metres high, off the southeast point has a clear passage inshore.

Stac a Mheadais, 24 metres high, stands close to the shore about 1 mile northwest of the entrance.

Fish traps extend south from the north point of the entrance.

Some shelter beyond the bend, off the northwest shore but the holding here has been found to be poor.

Good shelter and holding have been found in a gale from east and northeast close to the wooded shore on the east side at the corner.

Loch Harport

Waypoint ½ mile west of Ru na Clach 57°18'·6N 6°14'·8W

A branch of Loch Bracadale, described below, although Loch Harport is more conveniently treated as a separate loch.

Tidal streams are insignificant, and the loch is free from hidden dangers.

Light

Ardtreck Point light beacon Iso.4s17m9M

Anchorages

Oronsay, west of Ardtreck, gives some shelter on the east side of the drying reef which joins the island to Skye.

A drying reef extends ½ cable southeast from the northeast point of the island.

The best landing place is reported to be in the SW bay on the SE side of Ullinish Point.

Meals and showers at Ullinish hotel; advance booking is requested.

Loch Beg, northeast of the entrance is a satisfactory anchorage only if there is no sea from the south. The bottom is soft and the holding has been found to be poor.

Several inshore fishing boats lie on moorings, and the end of a concrete slip on the west side is marked by a prominent perch.

Shop, restaurant and post office up hill at the main road.

Gesto Bay, the next bay to the east, is good in offshore winds.

Portnalong, on the south side of the loch, opposite Loch Beg, provides better shelter in southerly winds.

Many inshore fishing boats lie on moorings, and the west side is occupied by fish cages. Anchor between the moorings and the fish cages. A jetty lies at the east side of the entrance, consisting of a sloping deck on broadly-spaced piles; there is depth to go alongside at all states of the tide but it is not suitable to remain there.

Post office, telephone, hotel, all ½ mile along road; shop nearly a mile away. Showers at 'The Bothy' bunkhouse, also cycle hire. *Calor Gas* at hotel.

Carbost, on the south shore, 1½ miles from the head of the loch.

A shoal area extends out from the distillery burn, and there is a broader area with moderate depth beyond the shoal, below a war memorial, but the head of the loch dries off for nearly a mile.

Anchor near the southwest shore between the pier and the distillery.

Green-painted visitors' moorings are laid off the Old Inn, ESE of the distillery. Do not mistake a buoy (also green), marking an outfall from the distillery, for these.

The pier has a depth of about 2 metres alongside and is sometimes used by fishing boats; a yacht would need fender boards at the pier.

Supplies

Shop at Carbost, post office, hotel (meals), telephone at hotel. Water from tap outside public toilet. Tours of distillery.

Loch Harport entrance: Ardtreck beacon on the right with Port na
Long beyond.

Loch Beg, Loch Harport from the head. The perch on the submerged end of the slip is on the right.

Carbost, looking ESE, towards the distillery. Visitors' moorings are beyond the anchored yachts

Loch Bracadale

57°20'N 6°32'W

Tides

Constant −0050 Ullapool (−0510 Dover)

Heights in metres

MHWS	MHWN	MTL	MLWN	MLWS
5·1	3·8	2·9	2·1	0·8

Dangers and marks

Rubha nan Clach, the southeast point of the entrance, is a cliff 129 metres high.

Wiay, in the middle of the entrance is 60 metres high, flat-topped with cliffs all round.

Idrigill Point, the west side of the entrance, is identified by Macleod's Maidens, three rock stacks standing close southwest of it.

The outer part of the loch is free from hidden dangers and, although it has several branches, there is little shelter.

Anchorages

Oronsay The bay on its northwest side is clean but very restricted.

Tarner Island gives some shelter on its northeast side.

Loch Caroy, north of Wiay, provides little shelter.

Tarner Island, ¾ mile north of Wiay, may be passed on either side but, if on the east side, keep closer to Tarner than to Skye as drying rocks lie in the middle and to the east side of the passage.

Sgeir a' Chuain, 2 metres high, ¾ mile further north has drying reefs up to a cable round it, but can be passed on either side.

About ¼ mile north of Sgeir a' Chuain, drying reefs extend 2 cables from Crossinish Point on the west shore.

Anchor near the jetty on the east side, ½ mile from the head of the loch.

Loch Vatten is entered by the west side of Harlosh Island, 1½ miles northwest of Wiay.

Harlosh Skerry dries 2 cables west of Harlosh Point.

Loch Bharcasaig, Loch Bracadale.

Poll Roag at the head of Loch Vatten can only be entered near HW by shallow-draught boats, but is traditionally a winter mooring for fishing boats. Holding is poor with weed and patches of soft mud.

Loch Bharcasaig, an inlet on the northwest side of Loch Vatten, with a forestry plantation at its head, is the best anchorage in Loch Bracadale other than Loch Harport; anchor in the southwest corner in 4 metres. Drying rocks lie ¼ cable off the south point of the entrance.

Northwest coast of Skye from Neist Point to Rubha Hunish

The northwest coast of Skye is deeply indented, with extensive groups of lochs between Dunvegan Head and Waternish Point and the west side of Trotternish. There are no hidden dangers on a direct passage between Neist Point and Rubha Hunish.

Waypoint 1 mile WNW of Waternish Point 57°37'·3N 6°39'·2W

Charts
1795 (1:100,000)
OS map *23*

Tides
Tides at Neist Point are described on page 47.

Between Neist Point and Ru Bornesketaig, 6 miles southwest of the north end of Skye, streams run at up to 1½ knots.

The north-going stream begins −0405 Ullapool (+0400 Dover).

The south-going stream begins +0220 Ullapool (−0200 Dover).

At Waternish Point the tide turns 15 minutes later and runs at 2½ knots. Overfalls occur off Waternish Point.

Dangers and marks
Dunvegan Head is 310 metres high with cliffs on its northwest side sloping down to the north.
  A conspicuous radio mast stands 3 miles south of the head.
  Waternish Point is 15 metres high, with a white light beacon 7 metres in height at the point.
  An t-Iasgair, an islet 21 metres high, lies 1½ miles NNW of Rudha Bornesketaig.

Lights
Neist Point Fl.5s43m16M
Waternish Point Fl.20s21m8M
Eilean Troddaay Fl(2)WRG.10s49m12-9M

Shelter

Loch Dunvegan, Loch Snizort, Duntulm Bay (limited).

Loch Pooltiel

57°28'N 6°45'W

Exposed northwest but, in moderate weather, small boats can anchor between the pier at Meanish on the west side of the loch and Sgeir Mor, a broad drying rock 1 cable southeast of the pier.

A rock with less than 2 metres depth lies about 1¼ cable northwest of the pier.

The bottom appears to consist of boulders.

Small-boat moorings lie southeast of the pier.

The head of the loch has been found to have good holding in firm mud, 3-5 metres, but dries off for several cables.

Many fishing floats and fish cages lie in the loch.

Supplies

Shop, licensed restaurant, post office, telephone, at Glendale at head of the loch. Telephone at Milovaig, uphill from pier. A working watermill maybe visited at Glendale.

Loch Pooltiel: anchorage at the pier from south.

Loch Dunvegan

57°30'N 6°40'W

Charts

2533 (1:25,000)
OS map *23*

Tides

Constant −0045 Ullapool (−0505 Dover)

Height in metres

MHWS	MHWN	MTL	MLWN	MLWS
5·2	3·8	2·9	1·1	0·7

Dangers and marks

Groban na Sgeire is the peninsula which separates Loch Dunvegan from Loch Bay.

A drying reef extends more than 2 cables SSW from Lampay Islands, 2 cables west of Groban na Sgeire. Ard Mor open west of Isay, bearing 360° astern, leads clear of this reef.

Fishing floats are scattered throughout Loch Dunvegan.

2½ miles SSE of Lampay the channel is reduced to 2 cables between Fiadhairt, a peninsula on its northeast side, and Eilean Grianal 7 metres high, with a line of rocks on the southwest side.

Uiginish Point, a mile southeast of Fiadhairt Point, has a white light beacon 5 metres in height at its end.

A white church tower at Dunvegan village in line with the northwest side of Uiginish Point 128° leads along the middle of the channel.

A G conical buoy south of Gairbh Eilean lies on the north side of Bo na Famachd over which the depth is 0·9 metres; if passing southwest of it, keep closer to the shore than to the buoy.

Lights

Uiginish Point Fl.WG.3s14m7/5M (white 128°-306° but obscured by Fiadhairt Point when bearing more than 148°)
Pier head 2F.R(vert) occasional

At night

Keep in the white sector of Uiginish Point light, after which the lights of the village and pier are the only guides.

Dunvegan

The pier has been restored and is usable; dues are charged.

Visitors' moorings have been laid between the pier and the church.

If not using a mooring, anchor abreast of the church clear of moorings.

The bottom between the pier and the moorings is very soft and, beyond the hotel it is too shallow for

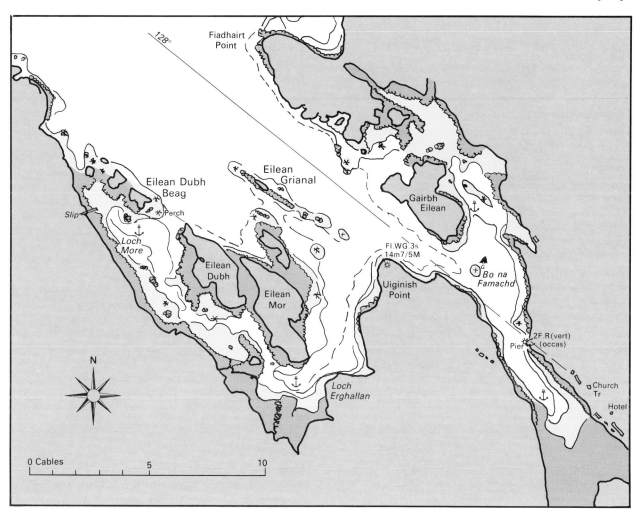

Loch Dunvegan (inner part)

most yachts, but good anchorage can be found there and *Thomasina* (11m c/b yawl) has ridden out a succession of summer gales there.

The jetty at Dunvegan Hotel is reported to be still unfinished, and dangerous framing, usually submerged, extends beyond the visible end of it.

Supplies at Dunvegan

Shops (including greengrocer and baker), post office, telephone, hotels and restaurants.

Petrol and diesel at garages; gas and gas fittings at garage. DIY/builders' merchant. Laundrette at caravan site.

Loch Mor, Loch Dunvegan, from northwest.

Gaeltec, an electronics firm, may be willing to help with electronic repairs and light machining in emergencies.

Diver at Stein ☎ 01470 592219, marine engineer at Uig ☎ 01470 542300.

Other anchorages

Gairbh Eilean Anchor between the castle and the island clear of rocks above water and drying which lie further north.

Loch More, 57°27'N 6°38'W, behind Eilean Dubh Beag off the southwest shore.

Clach a' Charra on the northwest side of the entrance is marked by a red perch with a T-shaped head, and rarely covers.

Below half-tide a drying rock southwest of Eilean Dubh Beag will be visible, and better shelter can then be found ESE of the slip at Colbost (which *is* public although you may be told otherwise).

Restaurant 1 mile south from slip.

Loch Erghallan, 57°26'N 6°37'W. Keep on the 128° line until within a cable of Uiginish Point to avoid Bo Channanich; turn to starboard and anchor not more than a cable south of Eilean Mor.

Loch Bay
57°30'·5N 6°35'W

Tides *as Loch Dunvegan*

Dangers and marks

Three islands, Isay, Mingay and Clett, lie in the entrance to the loch.

The passage north of Clett is ¾ mile wide but Sgeir a' Chuain, which dries, extends ¼ mile north of Isay.

To clear Sgeir a' Chuain, keep the tangent of Dunvegan Head astern bearing not more than 240°, or Waternish Hall, a low white building next to the war memorial, open north of Clett, 090°.

Several drying rocks lie south of Isay with a passage 2 cables wide south of them.

A spit with a depth of 2·4 metres extending 1½ cables north of Groban na Sgeire at the south side of the entrance may cause momentary alarm.

If approaching Loch Bay by the south of Isay, keep Dunvegan Head bearing 280° astern and follow the south shore of the passage until the west side of Ardmore Point is open east of Mingay 338°.

Sgeir nam Biast, a reef 2 cables across, part of which is above water, lies ¾ mile east of the south end of Isay and ½ mile from the south shore.

Anchorages

Isay, between Isay and Mingay.

From north approach with the east side of Rubha Maol showing between Mingay and Clett 128° to

Stein, Loch Bay, from east. Rubha Maol is on the left and Sgeir nam Biast lies in front of Isay and Dunvegan Head.

clear Sgeir a' Chuain, or Waternish Hall open of Clett 090° as above, and turn in to the channel between the islands when the big ruined house on Isay is visible.

From south approach with the west side of Ardmore Point open east of Mingay 338° to clear the east side of rocks south of Isay.

Anchor between Isay and the south end of Mingay. May be lumpy with wind from north or south.

Ardmore Bay, at the north end of Loch Bay is well sheltered from north, but the holding is said to be poor; the west side of the bay is shoal.

Stein, on the east shore of the southeast part of the loch, SSE of the pier.

There are many local boats on moorings, as well as visitors' moorings.

Apart from the obvious westerly exposure, there is sufficient fetch to make this a very uncomfortable anchorage in strong south winds.

At the head of the loch there is space to anchor and shelter from southerly gales, in spite of fish cages moored there.

Supplies at Stein

Pub, restaurant. Shop, post office, telephone ¾ mile uphill. Diver ☎ 01470 592219.

Loch Snizort

57°35'N 6°30'W

Charts

1795 (1:100,000), *2533* (1:25,000)
OS map *23*

Tides

Constant −0030 Ullapool (−0450 Dover)

Height in metres

MHWS	MHWN	MTL	MLWN	MLWS
5·3	3·5	2·1	1·9	0·7

Ascrib Islands

These islands, 1¼ miles from the west side of the loch, are generally clean, but drying and submerged rocks extend 1¾ cables northwest of the southwest point of South Ascrib.

Very occasional anchorage may be found in the bight on the west side of Eilean Garave, where the bottom is sand outwith the 2-metre line.

A shallow landlocked pool lies northwest of the house on South Ascrib, and a shoal-draught boat might lie there at neaps with lines ashore.

Dangers

See also approach to individual anchorages.

Lights

Waternish Point Fl.20s21m8M
Uig Pier head Iso.WRG.4s9m7-4M

Anchorages

Aros Bay, 57°33'N 6°33'W, an open bay on the west side of the loch where, formerly, car ferries used to shelter when the weather was too wild for them to approach Uig.

Loch Diubaig, 57°30'N 6°27'·5W, occasional anchorage in an open bay in the southwest corner of Loch Snizort. Bottom sand with patches of weed.

Loch Greshornish, 57°30'N 6°26'W, gives the best shelter in Loch Snizort.

Drying rocks lie 1 cable west of the south end of Eilean Mor at the entrance, as well as 1½ cables north of Greshornish Point, the west side of the entrance, and ½ cable off the east side of Greshornish Point.

The clear passage west of Eilean Mor is ½ mile wide; the passage east of Eilean Mor is 3 cables wide with no hazards.

Large unlit fish cages lie at the mouth of the loch, and many shellfish lines obstruct most of the head.

Submerged and drying rocks lie ¾ cable from the east shore 2 miles south of Greshornish Point.

The east tangent of Greshornish Point in line with the west side of Eilean Mor 018° leads west of these rocks.

Shop, pub and swimming pool at Edinbane on the east shore.

Loch Snizort Beag, 57°29'N 6°20'W, gives some shelter 3 miles from its mouth, just within the middle arm, the head of which dries off for 1 mile.

A submerged rock, Beatson, at a depth of 1·2 metres lies near the east shore of the loch 1½ miles from the mouth.

Hotel at the head of the middle arm.

Loch Treaslane, the western arm, is also sheltered although the head also dries off for 4 cables, and both these branches have good holding on mud. Loch Eyre, the eastern arm, dries off completely.

Christie Rocks which dry 2·2 metres lie 1½ cables offshore, about a mile south of the south point of Uig Bay. Stack of Skudiburgh, ¾ mile north of Uig Bay, open of the land 360°, leads clear of these rocks.

Poll na h-Ealaidh, a small inlet southeast of Christie Rocks, provides some shelter in offshore winds.

Uig pier at low tide

Uig pier from the opposite side of the bay

Uig Bay

57°34'·5N 6°23'W

The terminal for the ferry to Harris and North Uist.

The long pier provides some shelter, but much of the bay inshore of it dries.

The pier is used by fishing boats morning and evening and it is not recommended for yachts to lie there overnight, although they can go alongside during the day.

At night

Approach in the white sector of the light at the pier and keep a good lookout for fishing boats.

Supplies

Petrol and diesel from garage at pier. Diesel and water at pier; ask locally or at ferry office at car park for operator. Small shop at pier, larger shop with post office at head of the loch. Telephone at pier. Hotels.

Marine engineer, Sandy Morrison ☎ 01470 542300.

Other anchorages

Camas Beag on the south side of Uig Bay is an alternative anchorage in southerly winds but is deep until close to the head.

Tulm Bay (Duntulm)

57°41'N 6°21'W

Charts

1795 (1:100,000), also on *2210* (1:50,000)
OS map *23*

Tides

Off Rubha Hunish the spring rate is 3 knots

The northeast-going stream begins −0405 Ullapool (+0400 Dover)

The southwest-going stream begins +0220 Ullapool (−0200 Dover)

Constant −0030 Ullapool (−0450 Dover)

Height in metres

MHWS	MHWN	MTL	MLWN	MLWS
5·3	3·5	3·1	1·9	0·7

Marks

A lattice-work communications tower stands on Cnoc Roll southeast of the bay.

An t-Iasgair, 22 metres high, lies 1½ miles offshore NNW of Ru Bornesketaig.

Tulm Island lies in the middle of the bay and the ruins of Duntulm Castle stand on Ru Meanish at the south point of the bay.

Tulm bay from south. Hotel at right foreground

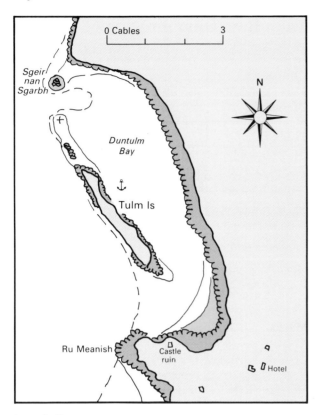

Duntulm Bay

Dangers

A drying reef extends about ½ cable southeast from the south end of Tulm Island, and drying reefs extend ½ cable west and northwest from Ru Meanish on Skye.

At the north end of Tulm Island a reef partly drying and partly submerged extends 1¾ cables NNW.

Sgeir nan Sgarbh which dries 4·6 metres lies near the Skye shore, with a narrow channel on either side of it.

A detached rock drying at LW lies just off the reef northeast of Sgeir nan Sgarbh.

Directions

Approach by the south entrance keeping midway between Tulm Island and Skye, heading 090° until the northeast side of Tulm Island is open.

From north, if Sgeir nan Sgarbh is visible either between the rock and the Skye shore – keeping rather closer to the rock – or ¼–½ cable south of the rock.

Anchor close to the northeast side of Tulm Island, north of the mid-point of the island, but this may be uncomfortable, as the tide may hold a yacht across the wind.

The bottom consists of sand with patches of weed.

A strong eddy is felt in the south part of the bay with south-going tides.

Services

Hotel.

Loch Ailort entrance (see page 17)
Photo: Jean Lawrence

Borrodale Islands from north, about high water. Druimindarroch at
bottom left and Eilean a' Cabar at left (see page 17)

Rudh' Arisaig (see page 21)

Arisaig Channel (see page 25)

Port Mor, Isle of Muck, from SSE near low water. Dubh Sgeir at lower left (see page 32)

Gallanach Bay, Muck, from NNW. Bohaund is just visible in the middle of the mouth of the bay (see page 33)

Canna Harbour. The buildings which serve as leading marks can be seen upper left (see page 38)

Hyskeir from SSE. Drying rocks lie in the bay northwest of the lighthouse (see page 38)

IV. Sound of Sleat and Loch Alsh

The Sound of Sleat and lochs on the mainland side are completely sheltered from the open sea, but surrounded by mountains and subject to severe squalls.

Charts
2208 (1:50,000)
OS map *33*

Tides
The northeast-going stream begins +0550 Ullapool (+0130 Dover).

The southwest-going stream begins −0010 Ullapool (−0430 Dover).

Dangers
On the Skye side of the sound, rocks above water and drying lie up to 2 cables offshore southeast and south of Armadale.

Tartar Rock, 4 miles NNE of Armadale with a depth of 1·5 metres, lies 2 cables offshore.

Off the mainland shore, submerged and drying rocks lie up to 2 cables NNE of Airor Island and, at the mouth of Glen Ghuserein, 1½ miles northwest of Airor, a bank dries off ¼ mile from the shore.

Conspicuous marks
Mallaig village at the southeast point of the entrance to the sound.

Armadale Pier, with a white building on its head.

Sandaig Island light beacon (north of Loch Hourn entrance) 12 metres high.

Isle Ornsay light tower, white, 18 metres high.

Lights
Sgeir Dhearg, Mallaig Fl(2)WG.8s6m5M
Mallaig Steamer Pier Iso.WRG.4s6m9-6M
Armadale Pier Oc.R.6s6m6M (not easily seen among shore lights)
Isle Ornsay Oc.8s18m15M 157°-vis-030°
Isle Ornsay north Fl.R.6s8m4M
Sandaig Island light beacon Fl.6s12m8M

At night
To clear dangers off Armadale keep Isle Ornsay light in sight bearing not more than 030°; to clear Tartar Rock, keep this light bearing not more than 025°.

To clear the land north of Loch Nevis keep the white sector of Sgeir Dhearg light at Mallaig in sight.

Shelter
Limited at: Glaschoille (Loch Nevis), Armadale, Isle Ornsay.

Loch Nevis
Waypoint ¼ m south of 1·2 metre rock 57°01'·3N 5°44'·7W

Charts
2541 (1:25,000), *1987* and later editions only
OS map *33*

Tides
Streams in the entrance south of Rubha Raonuill run at ½ knot; elsewhere they are weak except at the narrows where they run at 3 knots.

The in-going stream begins +0530 Ullapool (+0110 Dover)

The out-going stream begins −0050 Ullapool (−0510 Dover)

Constant −0040 Ullapool (−0500 Dover)

Height in metres

MHWS	MHWN	MTL	MLWN	MLWS
5·0	3·8	2·9	2·0	0·7

Dangers and marks
A white monumental statue stands near the southeast point of Rubha Raonuill.

Rocks, above water and drying, lie on the N side of the entrance between Eilean Glas and Rubha Raonuill.

Bogha cas Sruth which dries 1·8 metres, 3½ cables WSW of Rubha Raonuill, is the most dangerous. Inverie House just showing south of Rubha Raonuill 083° leads 1 cable south of Bogha cas Sruth.

A submerged rock lies more than a cable SSW of Rubha Raonuill at a depth of 1·2 metres; the beacon on Bogha Don in line with Inverie Church 075° leads close south of this rock.

Bogha Don, a drying rock 1½ cables southeast of Rubha Raonuill is marked by a tapered stone beacon with a cross topmark

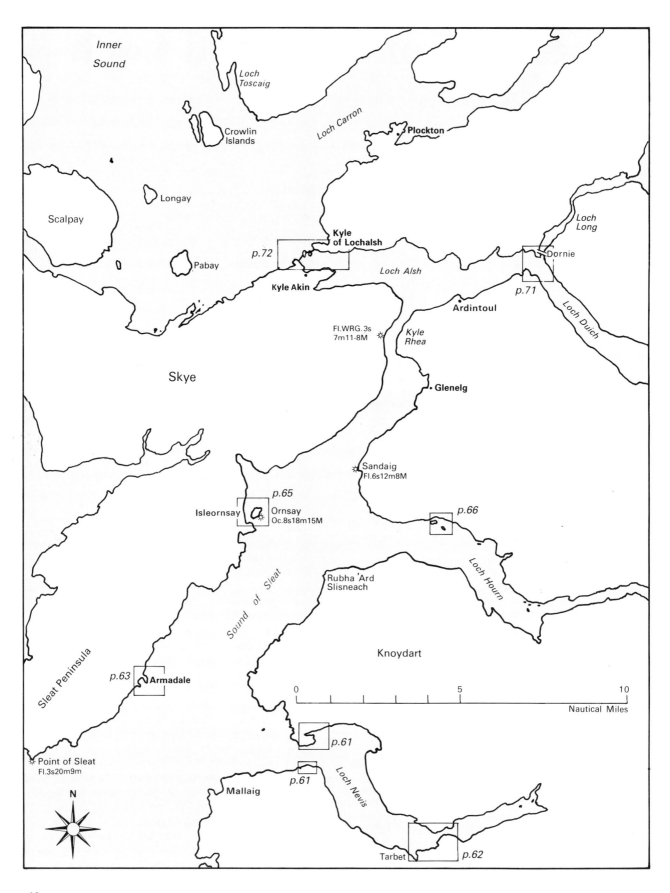

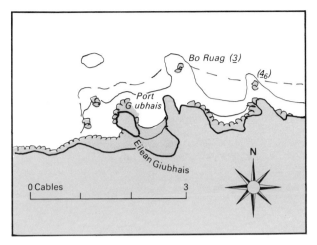

Port Giubhais

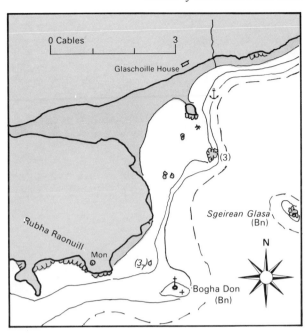

Glaschoille

On the south side of the loch, Bo Ruag dries 3 metres, ¾ cable offshore and about 3 cables west of Rubha na Moine, the point where the shore turns sharply to the south.

Anchorages

Port Giubhais, 57°01'N 5°44'·3W, on the east side of Eilean Giubhais provides occasional anchorage for small boats under a steep hillside on the south side of the loch.

Drying reefs extend northeast of Eilean Giubhais and a detached rock dries 1·2 metres northwest of Eilean Giubhais; Bo Ruag, described above, lies 1 cable ENE of the mouth of the inlet.

Glaschoille, 57°02'N 5°43'W, is particularly suitable in the northerly winds to which Mallaig is exposed.

Sgeirean Glasa is marked by a slim pole which is not easily seen at HW.

Drying reefs extend about ¼ cable northwest and southeast of Sgeirean Glasa beacon and other rocks lie further inshore.

The bay south of Glaschoille House and east of Eilean na Glaschoille is occupied by workboats on moorings, but space can usually be found to anchor among them. The bottom falls away steeply ½ cable from the low-water line. The seabed is sand and mud with some dense weed patches.

Inverie, 57°02'N 5°41'W, is in the northeast corner of the outer loch.

Anchor clear of moorings and the approach to the pier, but the holding is poor.

Visitors' moorings (15-ton capacity with pickups) have been provided by the proprietors of the pub.

The pier is constructed of concrete piles, with steps at its east side. Construction of a roll-on ferry terminal is planned (full details will be published in a future supplement).

Services and supplies

Shop, post office, telephone, water, *Calor Gas*, pub/restaurant, showers at pub, rubbish disposal,

ferry to Mallaig. Meals also at the Pier House if booked in advance.

Tarbet Bay, 56°58'·3N 5°38'W, on the south shore near the west end of the narrows.

Green huts belonging to an adventure centre stand on the shore of a bay west of Ardintigh Point, ½ mile west of Tarbet Bay, and a wooden house stands on Torr an Albannaich, the east point of the bay, with a flagstaff on an islet off the point; a drying rock lies ¼ cable west of the islet.

Lobster creels with floating lines are often moored in the bay; it is liable to be very squally, especially in southerly winds.

See colour photo between pages 90 and 91.

Loch Nevis Narrows, 56°59'N 5°37'W, is entered eastward of Torr an Albannaich (see above).

Roinn a' Chaolais, a long shoal spit, extends southwest from the north point of the entrance to the narrows and there are various drying rocks in and beyond the narrows.

Tidal streams run at 3 knots, turning as above.

Steer for the north side of Torr an Albannaich and when ½ cable from the shore steer for a white cottage on the south shore beyond Kylesmorar 065°.

Alter course again to keep in mid-channel at the beginning of the narrows, closing the north shore beyond the white cottage to avoid Sgeir an t-Sruith and a drying spit at the east end of the south side of the channel.

A shoal rock on the north side, 3 cables beyond the east end of the narrows is avoided by keeping Kylesknoydart cottage open south of the north point at the east end of the narrows 257°.

Drying rocks lie up to a cable off either shore.

At the head of the loch anchor either north or southeast of Eilean Maol as convenient clear of any moorings; the head of the loch dries for ½ mile.

61

Loch Nevis entrance

Tarbet Bay and the Narrows

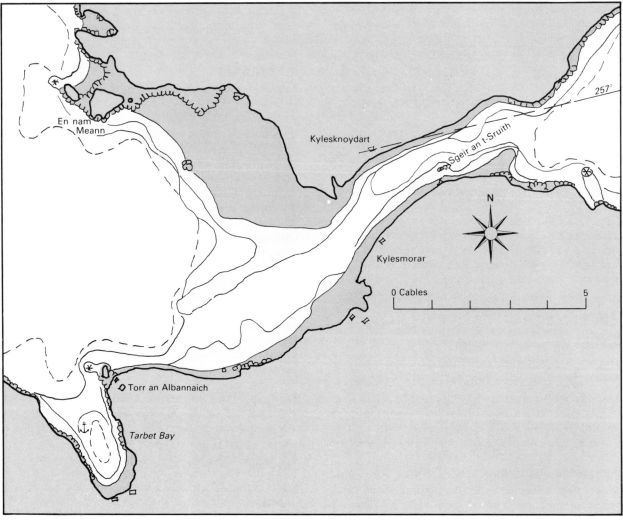

Eilean Giubhais, Loch Nevis. Rubha Raonuill beyond with Glaschoille House to the right

A new jetty has being built in the bay ½ mile west of Eilean Maol.

Occasional anchorages in Sound of Sleat

Sandaig Bay, 57°02'·5N 5°46'W, is an attractive daytime stop northeast of Glas Eilean at the mouth of Loch Nevis.

If coming from Loch Nevis the rocks on the east side should be carefully studied.

At the head of the bay a rock dries at half tide about a cable southeast of the islet there.

Doune (Dun Bane Bay), 57°04'N 5°47'·3W, a bay facing northwest a couple of miles north of Loch Nevis entrance.

Visitors' moorings are laid on the southwest side of the bay, sheltered from southwest by An Fraochaig. The east side of the bay is shoal inshore.

Services

Meals (booking requested by 5pm), showers, telephone, metfax, diver, repairs.

Water and diesel at the stone jetty on north side of promontory north of moorings; ask at house before going alongside.

Airor, 57°05'N 5°46'W, a shallow bay a mile northeast of Doune Bay, best visited at neaps or with a very shallow-draught boat.

The entrance between the island and a reef off the south point is only ½ cable wide and submerged rocks extend ½ cable southwest from the island.

Camas Daraich, 57°01'N 6°00'W, lies immediately east of Point of Sleat with a sandy beach at its head. *See colour photo facing page 90.*

A rock more than a cable from the west side of the bay dries at about half tide with a drying reef north of it and other drying rocks southwest.

Port na Long is a more open bay a mile east of Camas Daraich.

Acairseid an Rudha on the west side of the Sleat peninsula 7 cables north of the light beacon has a jetty and leading beacons, originally for servicing the light, but is probably best visited from the land.

Armadale

Waypoint ¼ mile NNE of Eilean Mhaol 57°03'·8N 5°53'W

Tides

Constant −0040 Ullapool (−0500 Dover)

Height in metres

MHWS	MHWN	MTL	MLWN	MLWS
5·0	3·8	2·9	2·0	0·7

Dangers and marks

Eilean Maol, 3 metres high, is the outermost of a group of rocks east of Ardvasar Promontory (Rubha Phoil), SSE of Armadale Pier.

A detached rock dries ½ cable NNE of Eilean

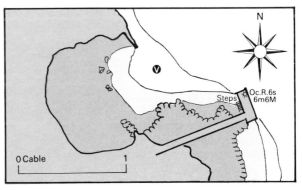

Armadale

Armadale   *Photo:* Mike Balmforth

Maol; the NNE face of the pier open leads clear of the detached rock.

Anchorage

Visitors' moorings are laid in the bay. Together with Sleat Marine Services' moorings, these leave little room for anchoring, but the bottom is firm sand.

It may be possible to leave a yacht in the care of Sleat Marine.

The bay is exposed to seas from northeast and in these conditions Knock Bay (see below) may be more comfortable.

A roll-on ferry terminal has been built at the north end of the Steamer Pier.

Lights

Armadale pier head shows Oc.R.6s6m6M, but is not easily picked out among the shore lights.

At night

When approaching from southwest, keep Isle Ornsay light in sight to clear Eilean Maol.

Services and supplies

Shop, hotel at Ardvasar (1 mile south), cafe, bar, takeaway and camping shop at pier.

Water at stone jetty on the north side of the bay. Diesel, emergency repairs to hull, engine and sails, and some chandlery, from Sleat Marine Services ☎ 01471 844216.

Doctor and district nurse.

Other anchorages

Knock Bay, 3 miles NNE of Armadale; the holding is said to be bad and the west side of the bay foul; the depth decreases suddenly from 18 to 1 metre.

Camas Croise, 57°08'N 5°48'W, has a bottom of stiff clay.

Isleornsay Harbour

57°08'·8N 5°47'·7W
See colour photo between pages 90 and 91.

Tides

Constant −0050 Ullapool (−0510 Dover)

Height in metres

MHWS	MHWN	MTL	MLWN	MLWS
4·8	3·7	2·7	1·6	0·7

Dangers and marks

A white lighthouse, 19 metres high, stands on Eilean Sionnach, a tidal islet southeast of Ornsay.

A grey stone light beacon stands on the northeast side of a reef off the north end of Ornsay, but part of the reef extends northwest of the beacon. Give the north shore of Ornsay a berth of at least a cable.

The bay shoals gradually towards its head and dries about a cable short of the pier.

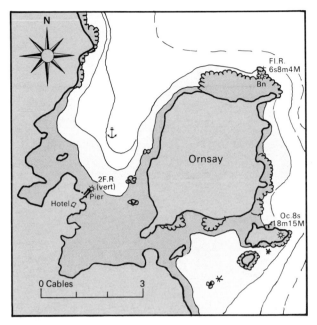

Isleornsay Harbour

Lights

Ornsay lighthouse Oc.8s18m15M
Ornsay Island light beacon Fl.R.6s8m4M
Pier head 2F.R(vert) and floodlights

Anchorages

There is said now to be little fishing-boat traffic, but a good anchor light should be shown. Salmon nets may be encountered on the west side of the bay.

Anchorage off Duisdale Hotel at the west side of the entrance is more out of the way and said to be more sheltered, as well as being a shorter distance to row ashore.

(Visitors' moorings had been laid some years ago but it is thought that they are not currently maintained.)

A bay on the west side, below a conspicuous church, has been found to provide good holding in a southerly gale, with no weed.

Supplies

Small shop at hotel by the pier. Post office, petrol, water tap. Baths at Duisdale Hotel.

Ornsay lighthouse

Other anchorages

Loch na Dal, 57°10'N 5°47'W, is a better anchorage in northerly winds.

Sgeir Ghobhlach stands above water on a coastal reef ¾ cable offshore on the north side of the entrance to Loch na Dal

Detached rocks, both drying and submerged, lie more than a cable from the shore in places up to 2 miles northeast of Sgeir Ghobhlach.

Loch Hourn

57°08'N 5°40'W

One of the most spectacular lochs in Scotland but subject to very high rainfall and severe squalls.

Charts

2541 (1:25,000)
OS map *33*

Tides

The in-going stream begins −0610 Ullapool (+0155 Dover)

The out-going stream begins +0005 Ullapool (−0415 Dover)

Streams run at 3 knots in narrows east of Corr Eileanan, with an eddy on the flood on the south side of the inner loch, but they are weak in the outer loch.

Constant −0110 Ullapool (−0530 Dover)

Height in metres

MHWS	MHWN	MTL	MLWN	MLWS
5·0	3·8	2·9	2·0	0·8

Dangers and marks

Sgeir Ulibhe, in the entrance of the loch about one-third of the width from the north side, dries 2·1 metres, with the remains of a metal beacon on it, and a rock just submerged lies a cable west of Sgeir Ulibhe.

Clansman Rock, halfway between Sgeir Ulibhe and the north shore, has a depth of only 2·1 metres over it.

Anchorages

Eilean Rarsaidh, 57°09'N 5°37'W, on the north shore of the outer loch has several drying rocks as on the plan which are not correctly shown on older copies of chart *2541*.

Anchor north or east of Eilean Rarsaidh. Shelter is said to be better than would appear from the chart and it is often preferred to Isleornsay.

Camas Ban, 57°08'N 5°34'W, Arnisdale. The bay is reported to be completely obstructed by moorings.

Eilean a' Phiobaire, 57°07'N 5°35'W. The passage and anchorage are reported to be completely blocked by a fish farm.

Eilean Rarsaidh, Loch Hourn, from north.

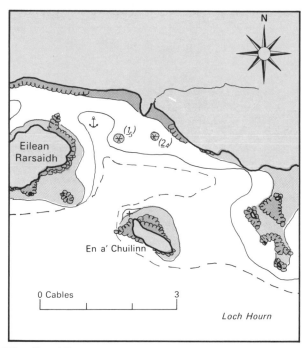

Eilean Rarsaidh

Loch Hourn: fish farming at Eilean a'Piobhaire

Poll a' Mhuineil, 57°06'N 5°34'W, is deep until close to the head of the pool and subject to severe squalls from south.

Loch Hourn Beag
57°06'·6N 5°24'W

The upper part of Loch Hourn is reached through a sequence of narrow passages east of Corr Eileanan.

The head of Barrisdale Bay, south of Corr Eileanan, dries up to half a mile.

Ellice Shoal lies 4 cables west of the two southern Corr Eileanan, and Duncan Shoal lies 2 cables west of the north Corr Eilean.

Upper Loch Hourn from the north shore. Eilean a' Gharb-Iain is right of centre and Caolas Mor at upper left

The tortuous channel leading to Loch Hourn Beag, from the south shore at low water springs

The tide runs at 3 knots through the narrows east of Corr Eileanan.

The main passage lies south of Corr Eileanan, and the southwest shore should be kept between ¼–½ mile until the south point of the first narrows is open south of the south Corr Eilean.

Pass within 2 cables south of the south island and then steer to pass within a cable south of Eilean a' Gharb-Iain to avoid an extensive bank which dries off the south shore.

The passage between the north and middle Corr Eileanan is clear but the south side of Eilean a' Gharb-Iain must be kept in sight in the passage 085° to avoid Duncan and Ellice Shoals.

At Caolas Mor, 1¼ miles east of Corr Eileanan, the south shore should be kept ½ cable off to avoid an extensive bank which dries southwest of the promontory on the north side of the narrows.

At Eilean Mousker (Mhogh-sgeir), just over a mile ENE of Caolas Mor, the passage is south of the island, keeping closer to the island to avoid a drying bank off the south shore.

Island Rock, ½ cable east of the island, covers at half tide.

Caolas an Loch Bhig, 1¼ miles further east, lead to Loch Beag.

The channel winds around and is only 0·6 metres deep but, if the passage is taken on the last two hours of the flood, it should present little problem.

When you can see clear water through the middle of the entrance there is 2·4 metres in the channel. At this time Island Rock, east of Eilean Mhogh-sgeir, is just covered around half tide.

After passing the cottage at Skiary on the south shore outside the narrows, close the south shore when a ruined shed is abeam.

Keep about 20 metres from the south shore until you come to a weed-covered spit with two rocks on the shore above it; follow closely the edge of the spit until on a line between the two rocks and the west end of the beach on the north shore.

Follow close to the north shore and then along the edge of the shingle spit which extends from the north shore, until more than midway across the channel again and then make for the middle of Loch Beag.

The tidal stream runs at about 2 knots and tends to set a yacht off course.

Holding in Loch Beag is poor and the head of the loch dries out to a line from the steps on the south side to the ruins of a boathouse on the north side. In a westerly gale the best shelter is in a bight of the north shore north of Eilean Mhogh-sgeir.

Sandaig Bay
57°10'N 5°41'·5W

Lies 1½ miles north of the entrance to Loch Hourn (not to be confused with the bay of the same name north of the entrance to Loch Nevis) southeast of Sandaig Islands, on the northwest point of which is a light beacon.

Rocks, submerged and drying, lie up to 1½ cables southeast of the islands, and off Sgeir nan Eun the most southerly above-water rock.

A drying reef extends about a cable from Rubha Mor at the southeast point of the bay.

Good shelter in winds with any northerly component.

Glenelg
57°12'·5N 5°38'W

On the east shore of Sound of Sleat, a mile southeast of the entrance to Kyle Rhea.

A monument stands on Rubha Mhic Cuinn and a submerged rock lies a cable west of Rubha Mhic Cuinn.

A wooden jetty lies a cable south of the promontory.

Anchor southwest of the jetty (the head of which covers at HW) clear of moorings, but the holding is poor.

A small pool, the entrance to which dries, where local boats are moored, lies north of the promontory.

Supplies

At Glenelg, ½ mile from the jetty: shop, post office, *Calor Gas*, petrol, hotel.

Kyle Rhea and Loch Alsh

Charts

2540 (1:20,000)
OS map *33*

Tides

Tidal streams in Kyle Rhea run at up to 8 knots and possibly more on occasions, with eddies along both sides; during the second half of the flood tide (north-going) the stream sets onto rocks on the west side of the channel.

At the south entrance to the kyle a southerly wind and ebb tide set up dangerous overfalls.

An eddy forms in Bernera Bay southeast of the south entrance on the south-going tide.

During the second half of the flood the stream sets across rocks on the west shore which are covered.

The stream runs at its fastest in the south entrance to the kyle.

The north-going stream begins +0600 Ullapool (+0140 Dover)

The south-going stream begins at HW Ullapool (−0420 Dover)

Dangers and marks

Drying rocks extend up to ¾ cable off both shores of Kyle Rhea.

A light beacon stands on the west shore of the kyle.

Sgeir na Caillich, nearly 2 cables north of the west point of the north entrance, is marked by a concrete pillar 2 metres in height.

Directions

Keep in mid-channel. If tacking beware eddies inshore.

Coming south, if the wind is southerly, beware overfalls ½ mile south of the entrance near the west shore. The worst can be avoided by steering for the southeast shore until clear south of a line between Dunan Ruadh and Glenelg village.

Anchorages

To wait for the tide at the south end, anchor off the jetty at Glenelg (see above) or on the west shore, north of a cable beacon standing 3½ cables south of the mouth of Kylerhea River. A drying bank extends nearly 2 cables from the river mouth.

At the north end anchor not less than 1½ cable WNW of Sgeir na Caillich beacon to avoid submerged rocks (although, with the large-scale chart, space can be found closer to the shore).

Lights

Kyle Rhea light beacon Fl.WRG.3s7m11-8M
Sgeir na Caillich light beacon Fl(2)R.6s3m4M

At night

The white sectors of Kyle Rhea light beacon lead through the entrances to the kyle.

Supplies

At Glenelg (see page 68).

East Loch Alsh and Loch Duich

Charts

2541 (1:25,000 and 1:12,500)
OS map *33*

Tides in East Loch Alsh

The in-going stream begins −0610 Ullapool (+0155 Dover)

The out-going stream begins −0005 Ullapool (−0425 Dover)

Constant −0025 Ullapool (−0445 Dover)

Height in metres

MHWS	MHWN	MTL	MLWN	MLWS
5·3	3·8	3·0	2·1	0·7

Entering Loch Duich. Totaig is in front of the promontory on the right

Eilean Donnan Castle, Loch Duich, looking WSW towards
Totaig (Ob Aonaidh)

Dangers and marks

Glas Eilean, 6 metres high with extensive drying
banks all round it, lies in the middle of the entrance
to the east part of Loch Alsh.

In the channel to the north of Glas Eilean, Racoon
Rock, at a depth of 1·8 metres, is marked by a green
conical buoy on its northwest side.

Rocks, awash and drying, extend more than ½
cable from the shore northwest of Racoon Rock
leaving less than a cable between them and the
buoy.

A drying bank on the north side of Glas Eilean
encroaches on a direct line between the buoy and
Eilean Aoinidh, a promontory on the south shore
1½ miles east of Glas Eilean, and a detached drying
reef lies 4 cables east of the north part of Glas
Eilean.

The channel south of Glas Eilean has drying banks
on both sides extending up to 1½ cables in places.

In the approach from west a drying bank extends
a cable north of Ardintoul Point.

A submerged rock lies more than a cable east of
Glas Eilean on the north side of the channel.

Do not approach Ardintoul Point to a depth of
less than 10 metres and, thereafter, keep equidistant
between visible shorelines.

The low water lines of Glas Eilean and Ardintoul
Point in line lead south of the rock east of Glas
Eilean.

Anchorages

Avernish Bay, north of Glas Eilean, although
obstructed by underwater cables, is useful for shelter
in strong east or northeast winds.

Ardintoul Bay, southwest of Glas Eilean, is
occupied by fish cages, but there may be space to
anchor inshore of them.

Loch Duich is entered between Eilean Aoinidh, a
rocky wooded point on the south shore, and Eilean
Tioram, which is low and grassy, on the north side.

The foreshore of Eilean Tioram dries off 2 cables
on the west side and ¾ cable on other sides.

Aile More Bank at a depth of 1·8 metres lies in the
middle of the loch, 3 cables east of Eilean Aoinidh.

Eilean Donnan Castle is conspicuous on the
northeast shore at the east side of the entrance to
Loch Long.

Many fish cages are moored off the southwest
shore of the loch.

Ob Aoinidh (Totaig), 57°16′N 5°31′·5W, is a
small bay on the east side of the peninsula named
Eilean Aoinidh.

It is surrounded by trees and an extensive reef,
partly above water, lies in the middle of the bay.

The bottom is rather hard so that an anchor does
not dig in easily and the current runs strongly round
the bay, apparently continuously anti-clockwise at
some states of the tide, at other times clockwise on
the flood and anticlockwise with the ebb.

Several moorings restrict anchoring space.

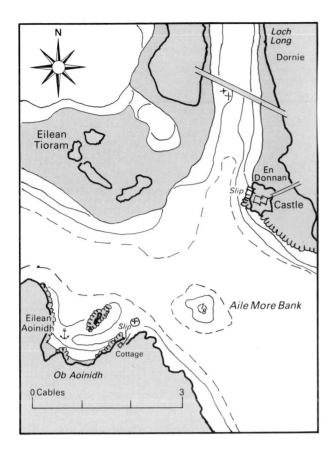

A rocky shelf extends east of the north point of Eilean Aoinidh but, further south, the west shore of the bay is steep-to and a line can be taken ashore to restrict swinging and hold a yacht out of the worst of the tide.

A rock awash lies less than ¼ cable off the old ferry cottage at the east point of the bay.

Water may be available from a tap at the ferry cottage.

Letterfearn Boat Hire, less than a mile southeast of Totaig, has moorings for hire.

Dornie, 57°17'N 5°31'W, at the mouth of Loch Long northeast of Eilean Aoinidh, is an occasional anchorage for buying stores or visiting the castle, but the tide runs strongly into and out of Loch Long. The bridge across the mouth of Loch Long has restricted headroom. Anchor off a slip on the northwest side of the castle.

Shops, hotels, post office, telephone, petrol, gas.

Anchorages at the head of the Loch

Ratagan Bay, 57°13'·2N 5°26'·5W, southeast of a promontory which lies southeast of Ratagan Youth Hostel, a prominent white building.

The head of the bay dries out 4 cables but, on the southwest side, a depth of 5 metres can be found a cable from the shore, and good shelter has been found there.

Invershiel Anchor off a concrete slip by the hotel on the east side of Bay of Invershiel.

Post office, telephone, hotel, petrol and diesel. Baths at hotel. Shop at Shiel Bridge, ¾ mile.

Loch Alsh, west part

Chart
2540 (1:20,000)

Dangers and marks
A submerged wreck, 2 cables off the south shore of Loch Alsh between Kyle Rhea and Kyle Akin, lies north of a group of fish cages, marked by east and west cardinal light buoys.

In Scalpaidh Bay, ½ mile ENE of Eileanan Dubha, a rock which dries 0·8 metres lies more than a cable offshore.

Lights
Sgeir na Caillich light beacon Fl(2)R.6s3m4M
South shore, E card Q(3)10s
South shore, W card Q(9)15s

Anchorages
The following bays on the north side of Loch Alsh have been used for anchoring under appropriate conditions.

Aird a Mhill Bay, 57°16'·5N 5°36'W, provides some shelter in easterly winds but the head of the bay dries off 1 cable and the bottom drops rapidly to more than 30 metres. Anchor in 5 metres just east of the mouth of the burn.

Balmacara Bay, 57°17'N 5°39'W, anchor towards the west side of the bay east of a jetty below trees. The rest of the bay dries off for 1 cable.

Hotel and pub. Visitors' moorings.

Scalpaidh Bay, 57°17'N 5°41'·5W. Anchor in 5 metres, sand with weed patches, in the western third of the bay, keeping well clear of the rock referred to above which dries 0·8 metres.

Loch na Beiste, 57°16'N 5°43'W, south of the east entrance to Kyle Akin is deep, and foul with old moorings, but a narrow shelf on the northwest side has suitable depths for anchoring and it is sheltered from all but easterly winds. Noted as being full of fish cages and buoys.

Kyle Akin
A narrow passage, in places only 1½ cables wide, linking Loch Alsh with the Inner Sound. A bridge with 30 metres headroom crosses the west end of the Kyle.

Charts
2540 (1:20,000 and 1:12,500), *2209* (1:50,000)
OS map *33*

String Rock Buoy Fishery Pier Ferry slip

Approach to Kyleakin.

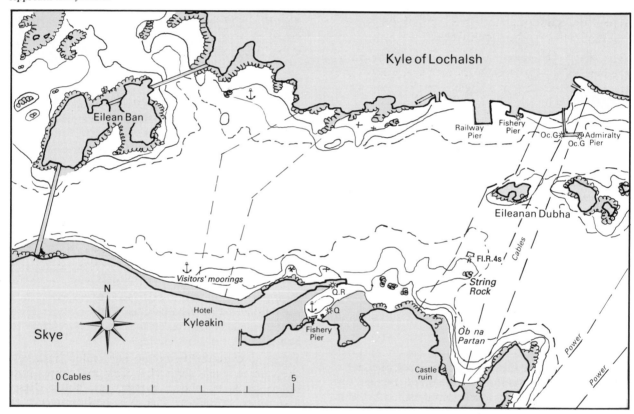

Tides

Tidal streams in Kyle Akin vary widely between springs and neaps, and are affected by barometric pressure, wind direction, rain and melting snow.

At neaps, the wind in particular may reverse the direction of flow, a southerly or southwest wind tending towards a west-going stream, and a northerly wind tending towards an east-going stream.

To present the information as simply as possible, perhaps over-simplifying it:

The east-going stream begins −0300 Ullapool (+0050 Dover) at springs, and +0100 Ullapool (−0320 Dover) at neaps

The west-going stream begins +0330 Ullapool (−0050 Dover) at springs and −0600 Ullapool (+0110 Dover) at neaps.

The west-going stream is usually the stronger, running at up to 4 knots at an extra spring tide.

For more detail see the *Admiralty Pilot*.

Constant −0030 Ullapool (−0450 Dover)

Height in metres

MHWS	MHWN	MTL	MLWN	MLWS
5·3	3·9	3·0	2·2	0·8

Dangers and marks

Eileanan Dubha are a group of islands at the east end of the kyle, north of mid-channel, marked by a white lattice light beacon 9 metres in height on their south side.

Off Rubha Ard Tresnish, the point of Skye south of Eileanan Dubha, a drying reef extends ½ cable.

String Rock which dries, 1½ cables off the south shore 1¾ cables southwest of Eileanan Dubha, is marked by a red can light buoy.

Drying rocks lie to the west of String Rock, up to 1½ cables from the shore.

North of Eileanan Dubha at Kyle of Lochalsh several jetties and piers project from the shore but the passage between the islands and the north shore is a cable wide.

Rocks, drying and submerged, lie up to ¾ cable from the shore west of Kyle of Lochalsh.

Kyle Akin lighthouse at the west end of the passage is entirely dwarfed by the bridge.

Black Eye Rock red can light buoy, 2 cables north of the head of a jetty at a quarry on Skye, west of the west entrance to the kyle, marks the most northeasterly of a patch of submerged rocks.

Bogha Beag, a reef which dries 0·6 metres, lies 3 cables WSW of the light buoy. Another red can light buoy lies 3½ cables west of *Black Eye Rock* light buoy.

Fork Rocks green conical light buoy ¼ mile northwest of the lighthouse, marks submerged rocks on the east side of the passage, and *Carrach* green conical light buoy, with a racon, lies 7 cables northwest of the lighthouse.

Note that a passenger ferry has been re-introduced into service across the Kyle.

Lights

Eileanan Dubha light beacon Fl(2)10s9m8M
Eileanan Dubha (West), south side Fl.G.6s5m5M
String Rock light buoy Fl.R.6s
Admiralty Jetty Oc.G.6s at each end of its head
Railway Pier 2F.G(vert) at each end of the head
  (listed 1996 as 'temporarily extinguished 1994')
Kyleakin Ferry Slipway Q.R
Dolphin Q

Lights at bridge

Oc.6s at mid-span, Iso.R.4s to SSW, Iso.G.4s to
  NNE, Q.Y at either side of fairway
Blackeye Rock light buoy Fl.R.6s
Bow Rock light buoy Fl(2)R.12s
Quarry jetty 2F.R(vert)
Fork Rocks light buoy Fl.G.6s
Carrach light buoy Fl(2)G.12s

At night

The succession of lateral buoys makes the passage relatively straightforward. Note that the Q.R light at Kyleakin slipway is not visible from either entrance to the Kyle.

Anchorages

Kyleakin, 57°16'·4N 5°43'·5W. A small pool on the south side of Kyle Akin entered through a dredged channel between the ferry slip and a half-tide rock 1 cable east of it. Most of the inner part of the inlet dries, as well as the bay on its southeast side. *See colour photo facing page 106.*

A fishery pier with two dolphins stands on the south side of the pool and a mooring for the ferry lies in the middle of the pool.

A yacht should be able to anchor clear of the mooring or lie alongside other boats at the fishery pier or, at three-quarters flood, lie temporarily alongside the quay on the north side of the pool. It is noted that yachts may berth alongside a spare ferry at Kyleakin.

Supplies

Shops, post office, telephone, garage, gas, hotel. Visitors' moorings are laid north of Kyleakin, off the King's Arms Hotel; do not anchor to the east of the hotel as cables cross the kyle there. Disturbed by passing traffic, and by swell in northerly winds. The bottom is blue clay.

Ob na Partan, south of *String Rock* buoy, has cables running from the head of the bay to the mainland but, ½ cable from the west side, there is a depth of 7 metres clear of the cables.

Kyle of Lochalsh
57°16'·8N 5°42'·7W

To go ashore for stores, berth at the east side of the Railway Pier where dues are charged, or at the Fishery Pier, which is of open-pile construction and subject to disturbance from fishing boats. Pontoons for use by day and restricted use overnight in settled weather are being installed in 1997.

Supplies

Shops (including butcher, baker and a hardware shop which stocks some chandlery and paint), post office, bank, telephone, garage, gas, hotel. Diesel and water at Railway Pier (see harbourmaster at portakabin on pier, or call him on Ch 16 or 11).

Tourist information office. Doctor, dentist, chemist. General marine and electronic repairs. Showers at car park. Swimming pool.

Anchorage

The bay ½ mile west of Railway Pier is clear north of the cable area, with moderate depth for anchoring on sand with patches of weed.

Communications and traffic control

Larger vessels passing through the Kyle call *Kyle Harbour* on VHF channel 16 (working channel 11) when about 3 miles out, as they may be invisible to vessels heading the other way. This is not a compulsory scheme but both these channels should be watched by yachts; they may also call the harbour office for information about traffic. HM ☎ 01599 534167.

V. The Inner Sound

The Inner Sound, which extends some 20 miles from Broadford Bay to the north end of Rona, together with the Sound of Raasay and Loch Carron, provides an area of sheltered water with spectacular scenery and a wide variety of anchorages; Lochs Torridon and Gairloch may be reached without rounding a major headland.

Cloud caps blowing off the Skye hills are taken to indicate imminent squalls.

Charts
2209, 2210 (1:50,000)

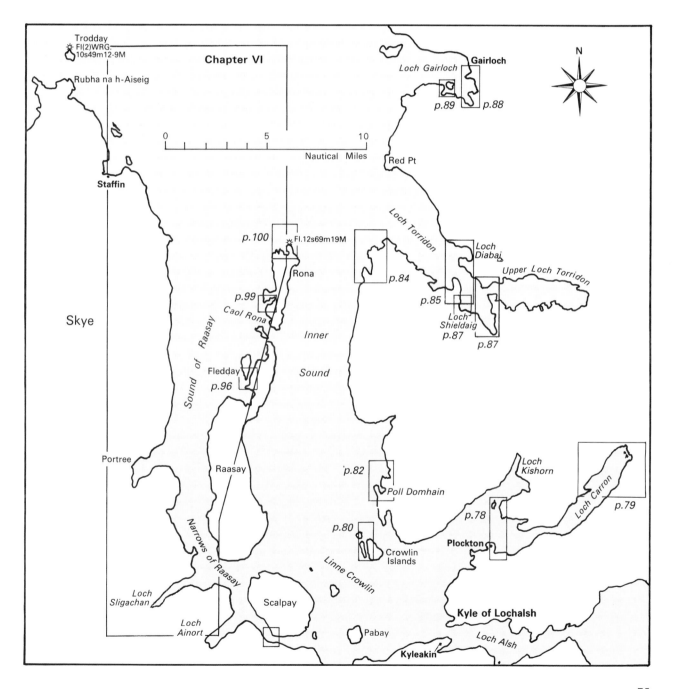

Loch Carron (outer part) and Loch Kishorn

57°21'N 5°42'W

Charts

2498 (1:25,000), 2528 (1:15,000)
OS map *24*

Tides

Tidal streams are negligible.

Constant −0010 Ullapool (−0430 Dover)

Height in metres

MHWS	MHWN	MTL	MLWN	MLWS
5·1	3·8	2·9	2·0	0·7

The northwest side of the loch is clean and steep-to, but the southeast side is indented with many bays (some of which are suitable for occasional anchorage), with offlying islands and drying rocks.

A course from the green light buoy, 7 cables northwest of Kyle Akin lighthouse, towards An Dubh-aird, a promontory 4 miles northeast, keeping two cables off each island and point, passes clear of all hidden dangers (although a drying reef southwest of Black Islands, ¾ mile NNE of the light buoy, lies close to this line).

For the inner part of Loch Carron see page 78.

Lights

All lights in Loch Carron have been removed.

Minor anchorages

Camas an t-Strathaidh, 57°20'N 5°41'W, ¾ mile south of An Dubh-aird can be entered by either side of Eilean Dubh Dhurinish, the most northwesterly island in the entrance.

A drying reef extends more than a cable southwest and a submerged reef up to a cable ESE of the island.

The sides and head of the bay are shoal and drying, with drying rocks more than a cable from the shore.

Kishorn Island, 57°22'·5N 5°39'W. The anchorage is between the island and Rubha na h-Airde, the promontory on the south side of Loch Kishorn.

Drying rocks extend more than a cable SSW of the island, leaving a passage less than a cable wide between Kishorn Island and Garbh Eilean (Garra Islands).

If approaching from seaward, make for the middle of Garbh Eilean and keep less than ½ cable from that island; the approach by the north side of the island is safer.

Head of Loch Kishorn A reef drying 3·6 metres lies 4 cables from the east shore northwest of Achintraid village, and most of the area between the reef and the shore dries.

Anchor between the reef and a promontory 3 cables south of it. Alternatively, west of Ardarroch on the north side of the head of the loch, off boat houses northeast of an islet on the east side of the mouth of River Kishorn.

Shop, post office, garage (petrol and diesel) on main road about ¼ mile from Ardarroch.

Plockton

57°20'·5N 5°38'·5W

Tides

Tidal streams are negligible.

Constant −0020 Ullapool (−0440 Dover)

Height in metres

MHWS	MHWN	MTL	MLWN	MLWS
5·5	4·1	3·1	2·2	0·8

Creag Mhaol

Loch Carron approach.

Charts

2528 (1:15,000)

OS maps *24, 25*

Buoys and beacons

Established to meet the needs of the oil-rig construction yard at Loch Kishorn, all have now been removed and are unlikely to be restored unless further commercial use is made of the site.

Dangers and marks

Dangers and marks in the approach to Plockton are described below; those for the passage further up Loch Carron are described in later pages.

Cat Island (Eilean a' Chait) is a tidal islet on which stands a conspicuous white disused lighthouse, north of Rubha Mor, the promontory north of Plockton.

Drying rocks extend more than a cable northwest of rocks and islets standing above water between An Dubh-aird 1¼ miles WSW, and Cat Island.

The south tangent of Eilean an t-Sratha, the largest of Strome Islands (or alternatively the summit of Creag Mhaol, east of Strome Islands), open north of Cat Island 092°, leads clear of the most northerly of these drying rocks.

Sgeir Golach, an area of drying rocks about ¼ mile across, lies ¼ mile north of Cat Island.

High Stone, the southeast point of these rocks is 1 metre high, and an iron tripod beacon with a basket topmark stands on the southwest point.

A drying rock lies nearly ½ cable south of the line between the beacon and High Stone.

Sgeir Bhuidhe, 4 metres high, and Sgeir a' Chinn 1 metre high, lie about ¾ mile north of Cat Island.

Sgeir Beag, ¼ mile ENE of Sgeir Bhuidhe, dries 1·5 metres and is very dangerous if passing direct between Loch Kishorn and Plockton.

Hawk Rock, almost awash at LW lies ¾ cable

ENE of Cat Island. High Stone in line with Sgeir Bhuidhe, 330°, leads east of Hawk Rock.

Duncraig Castle, about ¾ mile SSE of Cat Island, is conspicuous.

Bogha Dubh Sgeir, on which is a beacon similar to that on Sgeir Golach, lies ½ mile east of Cat Island, with No. 2 red can light buoy south of it.

Plockton Rocks, drying at half tide, lie NNW of Sgeir Bhuidhe, an islet (different from the one of the same name above) off the southeast shore. High Stone, or the west side of Kishorn Island, in line with the east tangent of Rubha Mor, leads west of these rocks.

A drying reef lies nearly ½ cable off Roinn an Fhaing at Plockton village.

Directions

After passing An Dubh-aird, steer about 060° until Eilean an t-Sratha is clear open north of Cat Island; steer to pass between Cat Island and High Stone until High Stone is in line with Sgeir Bhuidhe, 330°. Steer to keep this line astern (or use the alternative transit above) until Rubha Mor is abeam and steer for Plockton village.

Anchorage

Anchor off the slip at the north end of the village if space can be found clear of moorings (as well as thick weed), or between the village and Duncraig Castle, clear of Plockton Rocks and Sailing Club starting line, indicated by a flagpole on shore and a chequered buoy in transit.

Supplies

Shop, hotels, telephones, *Calor Gas* from shop. Water from tap (hidden in an old pump inside a small fence on the village green), or from a tap at rear of toilets at car park; use of a hose may also be offered from house by the slip at the north end of the village. Showers at Plockton Hotel. Laundry at caravan site (¼ mile north of village). Diesel from Calum Mackenzie (Leisure Marine ☎ 01599 544306). Sailing club.

Plockton from south; Loch Kishorn upper right.

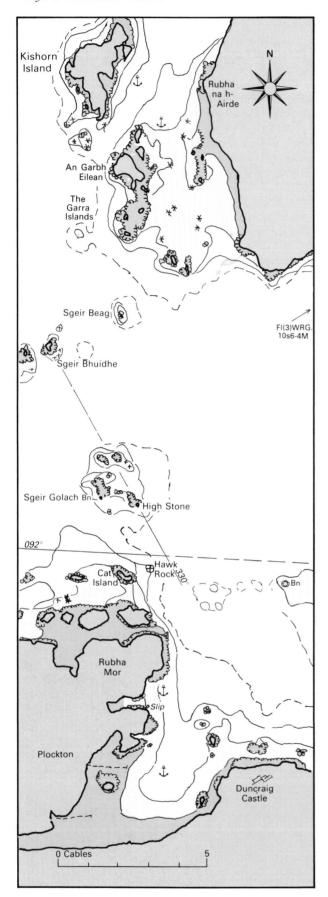

Strome Narrows and Inner Loch Carron

Charts
2528 (1:15,000) only as far east as Strome Narrows; for the inner loch use *2209*
OS maps *24, 25*

Tides
In Strome Narrows tidal streams run at up to 3 knots but are negligible elsewhere.

The in-going stream begins +0605 Ullapool (+0145 Dover)

The out-going stream begins +0005 Ullapool (−0415 Dover)

Constant −0010 Ullapool (−0430 Dover)

Height in metres

MHWS	MHWN	MTL	MLWN	MLWS
5·1	3·8	2·9	2·0	0·7

Dangers and marks
Bo Dubh Sgeir, ½ mile east of Cat Island, is marked by a beacon similar to that at Sgeir Golach.

Ulluva, 2 cables off the south shore, 7 cables southeast of Bo Dubh Sgeir, is marked by a stone cairn faded yellow in colour, and surrounded by drying rocks.

The bay to starboard dries off 2 cables and, at the narrows, a shoal area lies on the south side.

Directions
From the approach to Plockton, pass south of Bo Dubh Sgeir beacon, and two cables north of Ulluva island.

Lochcarron
Waypoint on leading line 328° 57°23'·5N 5°28'·6W

An extensive village on the northwest shore of the loch.

Slumbay Island, a peninsula at the south end of the village, partly shelters a bay known as Slumbay Harbour the shores of which dry off more than a cable. Slumbay Harbour is now full of moorings and a visiting yacht is unlikely to find space to anchor inside, although anchoring off the mouth is possible.

Sgeir Chreagach and Sgeir Fhada stand ½ mile offshore on drying reefs.

Red Rocks, some of which are submerged and some awash at LWS, lie between Slumbay Island and Sgeir Chreagach.

The foreshore in front of the village dries off in places up to ¼ mile; there is a drying area ¼ mile northeast of Sgeir Fhada, and the head of the loch dries off for 1 mile.

The approach between Sgeir Chreagach and Sgeir

Shed with green doors

Lochcarron: the shed with green doors above the village, in line
with a fence running up the hillside into a plantation bearing
328°, leads between Sgeir Creagach and Sgeir Fhada.
Photograph: Rob Teago

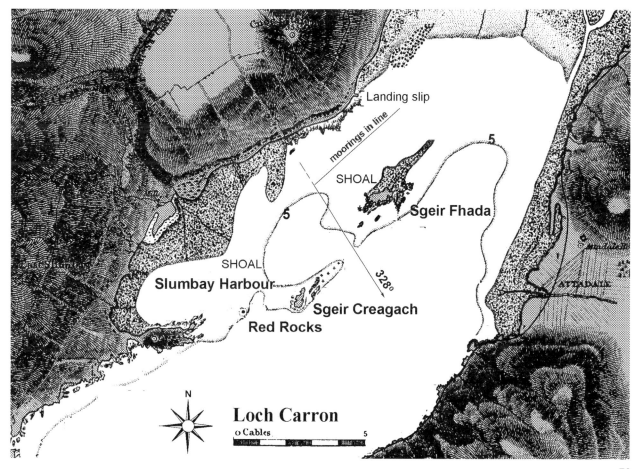

Landing slip

moorings in line

SHOAL

5

5

SHOAL

Sgeir Fhada

ATTADALE

328°

Slumbay Harbour

Sgeir Creagach

Red Rocks

N

Loch Carron

o Cables   5

Fhada is identified by the following line: a pale green shed with two dark green doors, bearing 328°, in line with a fence running up the hillside to the middle of a line of fir trees (see photo).

A jetty/slipway stands in front of the hotel north of Sgeir Fhada. Visitors' moorings (yellow, marked *visitor*) are laid in 3 metres off the jetty.

Approach

Leave Sgeir Creagach a cable to port, and turn onto the leading line 328° described above. When clear of the shoal water north of Sgeir Fhada, turn towards the moorings (these have been laid in line indicating the line on which to approach).

No formal charge is made for the moorings, but there is a box for donations towards maintenance costs in the hotel.

Supplies

Shops, post office, telephone, hotel, bank, medical centre.

Petrol, diesel and water at garage at head of jetty. *Calor Gas* at West End Garage. Bicycle hire.

Railway station 4 miles.

Slipping for dinghies and 'moderate sized' trailer sailers.

Drying out is possible alongside the old ferry slip at North Strome.

Caolas Mor

Waypoint 57°21'N 5°50'W

Charts

2480, 2498 (1:25,000)

Dangers and marks

In the passage northeast of Crowlin Islands, rocks submerged and drying on the northeast side of the passage extend 3½ cables south of Aird Mhor on the west side of Loch Toscaig. The northeast tangent of Eilean na Ba open of a 5-metre rock off the southwest side of Aird Mhor, 334°, leads close southwest of the outermost rock.

A rock which dries 1·1 metres lies 2 cables north of Eilean Beag, the most northwesterly of the Crowlin Islands, with other rocks between the drying rock and the island.

Fish cages east of the north end of Crowin Beag are marked by a yellow can light buoy.

Lights

A light beacon, Fl.6s32m6M, stands on the west
    side of Eilean Beag
Y can light buoy Fl.Y

Tides

In Caolas Mor tidal streams run at 1 knot at springs.

The southeast-going stream begins +0605 Ullapool (+0145 Dover)

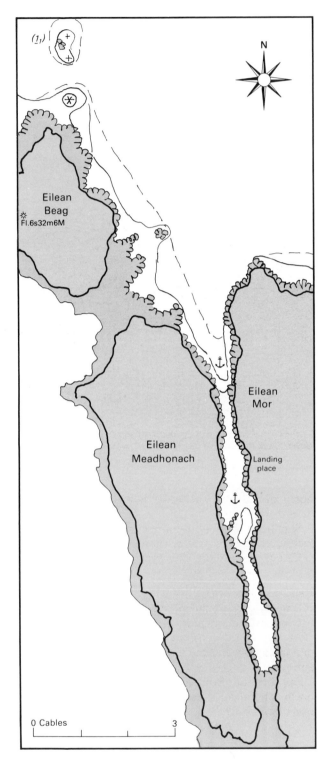

Crowlin Islands

The northwest-going stream begins +0005 Ullapool (−0415 Dover)

Anchorages

Loch Toscaig, 57°22'N 5°48'·5W. Occasional anchorage east or southeast of the pier.

In approach note the rocks described above; coming from west there is a clear passage 2 cables wide

Anchorage at the entrance to Crowlin Harbour

north of Bo Du, the most northerly rock, which dries 1·5 metres.

Shellfish-farming equipment on both sides of the loch is marked by orange buoys.

Camas na Ba on the west side of the loch is occupied by moorings.

Crowlin Harbour, 57°21'N 5°50'·6W, between Eilean Mor and Eilean Meadhonach, provides an occasional anchorage in its entrance.

Above half tide, the creek can be entered but most of it is shallow and the flood tide runs strongly in the entrance.

Approaching from the west, keep at least ¼ mile north of Eilean Beag to avoid the drying rock described above.

Poll Domhain and Poll Creadha

57°24'N 5°49'W

Charts

2480 (1:25,000)
OS map *24*

Tides

Constant −0015 Ullapool (−0435 Dover)

Height in metres

MHWS	MHWN	MTL	MLWN	MLWS
5·3	4·0	3·1	2·2	0·7

Poll Domhain

Poll Domhain is entered by the north side of Ard Ban which is identified by a conspicuous white beach on its west side.

Sgeir Mhor, which dries 3·2 metres 2 cables west of Ard Ban, is marked by a thin steel perch which is almost covered at HW. The high water line of the east side of Eilean na Ba in line with the east side of Eilean Mor (Crowlin Islands), 168°, leads west of Sgeir Mhor.

Drying reefs extend a cable north of Ard Ban. From northwest, pass south of An Ruadh Eilean. The head of the pool is narrowed by drying reefs on either side.

Extensive reefs lie on the west side of the inlet. The best landing place is on the west side of the more southerly reef.

Poll Creadha

Poll Creadha is obstructed by drying reefs, and safe access depends on the perches shown on the plan being in place. It should not be attempted if any swell is running.

A pair of white posts on shore used to mark the passage south of the central reef. The rear post has

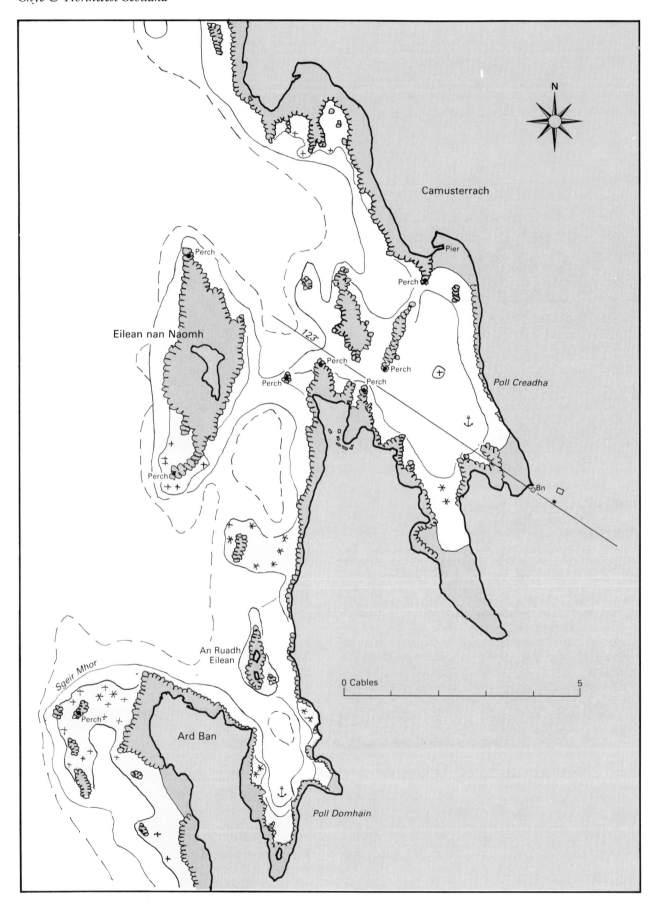

Camusterrach

Pier

Perch

Perch

Eilean nan Naomh

Perch

Perch

Perch

Perch

Perch

Perch

Poll Creadha

Bn

An Ruadh
Eilean

Sgeir Mhor

Perch

Ard Ban

0 Cables   5

Poll Domhain

Poll Domhain

Poll Creadha at low water springs. The perch off the end of the reef shows how difficult it would be to identify at high water.

been destroyed, but the remaining post just to the right of the right-hand corner of the second cottage from the left, bearing approximately 123° (see photo page 79), leads through the passage. Several poles which carry overhead cables might be confused with the post.

Supplies

None. Post office, shop and hotel at Applecross, 4 miles.

Inner Sound

The direction of buoyage throughout the Inner Sound and Sound of Raasay is northwards although the flood tide runs southwards.

Charts

2209, 2210 (1:50,000)
OS map *24*

Tides

In the Inner Sound the flood stream runs south, and spring rates are no more than 1 knot off headlands.

The south-going stream begins +0605 Ullapool (+0145 Dover)

The north-going stream begins −0005 Ullapool (−0415 Dover)

Communications

In any case, any vessel in Inner Sound is unable to communicate by VHF with Oban Coastguard – the Range Control (which watches Ch 13, 16 and 73 and is manned 24hr) will relay calls.

Dangers and marks

The fairway of Inner Sound is clean but, both in Caolas Mor, northeast of Crowlin Islands (above, page 80), and on a passage to Caol Mor between

Scalpay and Raasay (below, pages 91 and 92), there are specific dangers.

The Crowlin Islands, and Dun Caan on Raasay, the conspicuous plug of a former volcano, are useful reference marks.

An oil platform construction site south of Crowlin Islands, formerly marked by yellow buoys, has been discontinued.

Drying rocks lie up to 2 cables from the shore between ¾ and 1 mile south of the Range Control building (see below).

Underwater weapons-testing is carried out in a restricted area between Raasay and the mainland, marked by yellow pillar light buoys. Operations are controlled from the Range Control building at Ru na Lachan on the east shore 7 miles north of Crowlin Beag. The buoys are as follows:

C in mid-sound 3½ miles northwest of Crowlin Beag

D 5 cables off Raasay, 2¾ miles west of *C*

B about 1 mile NNW of the Range Control building.

Four special yellow buoys near the Range Control building mark a cable area.

When underwater testing is being carried out, a red flag is shown at the Range Control building (or, by night, a red light). A vessel approaching the restricted area will be contacted by VHF or by a patrol boat, usually a naval MFV. It is helpful for yachts approaching this area to call Range Control on VHF and listen to traffic on Ch 13. Yachts will be directed to pass clear of the restricted area to one side, usually the west. Information about each day's testing programme is broadcast on Ch 8 at 0800 and 1800.

Lights

Crowlin Islands light beacon Fl.6s32m6M
Eyre Point, Caol Mor Fl.WR.3s5m9/6M
Ru na Lachan Oc.WR.8s21m10M

Restricted area buoys:
C Fl.Y.5s
D Fl.Y.10s
B Fl.Y.10s

Cable area buoys off Range Control building
  Fl.Y.5s

Garbh Eilean (south end of Rona) Fl.3s

Various other light beacons on the east side of
  Rona have no navigational significance.

Rona lighthouse Fl.12s69m19M is obscured from
  358°-050°

Brochel

57°26'·5N 06°01'·4W
An occasional anchorage in bay below Brochel Castle near the north end of the east coast of Rassay. Look out for drying reef at the south end of the bay.

Ob Chuaig

57°26'·5N 06°01'·4W
An occasional anchorage south of the entrance to Loch Torridon, with a sandy beach at the head and several rocks in the bay (see plan).

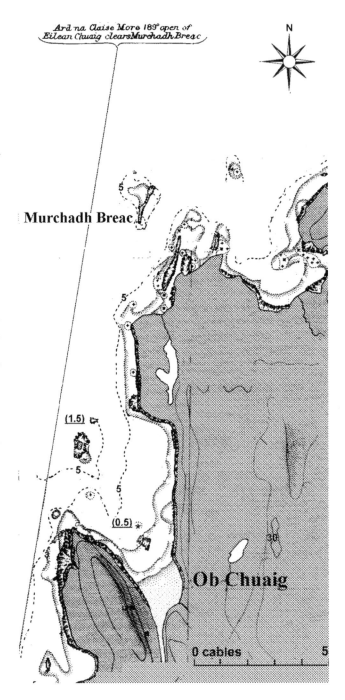

Loch Torridon

57°35'N 5°45'W

See colour photo between pages 90 and 91.

An impressive loch in three parts, joined by passages 4 and 2 cables wide, surrounded by spectacular mountains in its upper part.

Charts

2210 (1:50,000), obsolete chart *2638* (1:25,000) with depths in fathoms

OS *Outdoor Leisure Map* of Cuillin and Torridon Hills (1:25,000) shows useful detail in Upper Loch Torridon

OS map *24*

Tides

The in-going stream begins −0605 Ullapool (+0200 Dover)

The out-going stream begins −0005 Ullapool (−0425 Dover)

Constant −0020 Ullapool (−0440 Dover)

Height in metres

MHWS	MHWN	MTL	MLWN	MLWS
5·6	4·2	3·2	2·2	0·7

Dangers and marks in the outer loch

The entrance is 3 miles wide between Rubha na Fearn on the south side and Red Point on the north.

Murchadh Breac, 3 cables offshore, a mile west of Rubha na Fearn dries 1·5 metres and is a danger to yachts coming from south.

Murchadh Breac is cleared on its west side by keeping Ard na Claise Moire, a point 5 miles south, open west of Eilean Chuaig 187°.

The school house at Diabaig in Loch Torridon (the most southerly house there), open of Rubha na Fearn 098°, leads north of Murchadh Breac.

Sgeir a' Ghair, 1¼ cables northeast of Rubha na Fearn, is 0·5 metres high.

Sgeir na Trian, 2 metres high, lies 1¼ miles SSE of Red Point, towards the north side of the entrance and is in the way when coming from, or heading, north.

Sgeir Ghlas, 1 metre high, lies outside the mouth of a bay, 3 cables offshore 4 cables ESE of Red Point.

The southwest shore between Rubha na Fearn and Ardheslaig, the promontory on the south side of the

Ard na Claise More *open of* Eilean Chuaig *clears* Murchadh Breac
View *(at Lat. 57° 35'5 N., Long. 5° 50'5 W., approx.)*

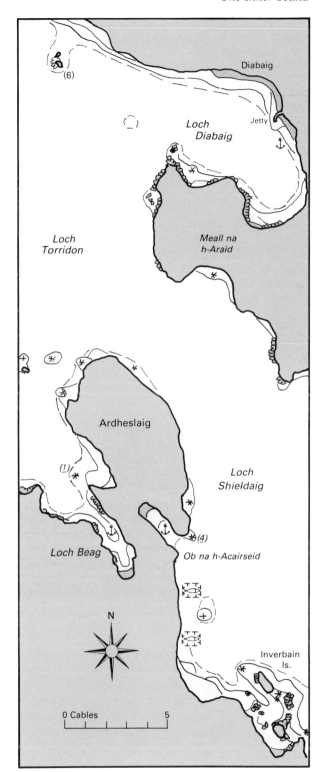

Loch Torridon

first narrows, is very broken with bays between rocky points and rocks which dry more than a cable from the shore.

The northeast shore is almost featureless as far as Rubha na h-Airde on the north side of the narrows.

Sgeir Dughall, 6 metres high, lies ¼ mile offshore 7 cables northwest of Rubha na h-Airde.

Ob Gorm Mor, Upper Loch Torridon   *Photo:* Wallace Clark

Minor anchorages in the outer loch

Camas Eilean, 1¼ miles west of Ardheslaig.

Occasional anchorage on the west or south side of the bay south of Eilean Mor. A fish cage is moored southeast of Eilean Mor; and the passage between Eilean Mor and the mainland is constricted by drying reefs.

Loch a' Chracaich, 57°33'N 5°44'W, a mile southwest of Ardheslaig.

Rocks drying 3 metres lie ½ cable east of Sgeir Glas off the north point of the bay, and submerged rocks lie about a cable from the south shore east of the mouth of a burn.

Fish cages are moored south of the north point and on the southeast side of the bay.

Anchor in the northwest corner, or at the south end of the southwest side of the bay; weed may be a problem. Telephone. No stores.

Loch Beag, 57°33'N 5°43'W, a narrow inlet ¾ mile south of Ardheslaig is occupied by fishing-boat moorings.

Dubh Sgeir, 2 metres high, lies ¼ mile west of Ardheslaig, northwest of the approach to the inlet.

A drying reef lies 1 ¼ cables ENE of Dubh Sgeir, and a submerged rock ½ cable NNW.

Other drying rocks lie near the shore further east.

A rock 1 cable northwest of the north point of Loch Beag dries 1 metre.

Rocks drying and submerged extend ¼ cable from either shore in places.

Several inshore fishing boats are moored in Loch Beag, but it is a useful alternative anchorage to Ob na h-Acairseid (see next page) in easterly winds.

Red Bay, 57°38'N 5°48'W, immediately east of Red Point, gives good shelter from northerly winds off a sandy beach.

Sgeir Ghlas, 1 metre high, lies 3 cables south of the middle of the head of the bay, and a submerged rock lies ½ cable west of it. Salmon nets and fishing floats lie in the bay.

Telephone 1½ miles along track.

Loch Diabaig, 57°34'·5N 5°42'W, lies on the northeast side of the outer loch, northeast of Rubha na h-Airde.

Sgeir Dughall, 6 metres high, stands 2 cables offshore ¾ mile northwest of Rubha na h-Airde.

The bay on the south side of the head of the loch is full of fish cages.

Anchor either side of the jetty, the head of which stands on a reef which covers at high water.

Loch Shieldaig

57°32'N 5°40'W

This is the middle part of Loch Torridon, with a good anchorage between Shieldaig village on the east side of the loch and Shieldaig Island, which is 41 metres high and thickly wooded.

Drying rocks extend 1 cable from the northwest point of the island and ½ cable north from its northeast side.

A rock ½ cable south of the point below the church at the north end of the village dries 2 metres.

The south end of the passage is blocked by drying and above-water rocks.

Supplies

Shops, post office, telephone, hotel. *Calor Gas* at Camas Doire Aonar on the west side of Loch Shieldaig.

Anchorages

The principal anchorage is southeast of Shieldaig Island, clear of the rocks described above.

The head of Loch Shieldaig dries for 2 cables and Sgeir Dhubh, in the middle of the loch 3½ cables from its head, dries 3 metres. Holding is said to be poor.

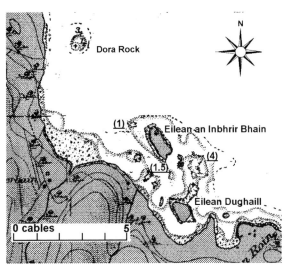

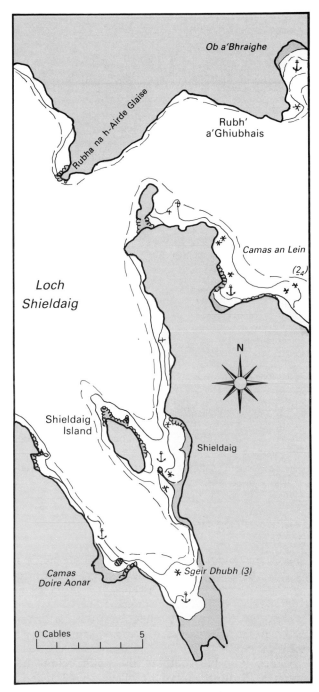

Loch Torridon

Inverbain Islands

southerly island and the mainland. There are two approaches: a channel from the northwest leads between the tidal islets and the mainland. At a distance of about 25m from the mainland coast the minimum depth is about 1m MLWS where there is a small spit and a stream enters the sea. An old mooring buoy, heavily coated with weed, in mid-channel looks suspiciously like a tidal rock. A second approach is south of the southerly island; there are indistinct leading marks. One is just above the beach at the left end of a small area of beach cleared of boulders and weed. The second mark is in trees and is not visible south of the leading line. The minimum depth is about 1·5m at MLWS. The anchorage has a depth of 1·5–2m at MLWS. The bottom is mud, a yacht appears to be permanently moored there and there is also a small pontoon with lobster gear. The latter is moored and also has a line ashore to the island.

Ob na h-Acairseid, 57°32'·5N 5°42'W, an inlet on the east side of Ardheslaig. Clean but very narrow.

Clach na Be, off the north point of the entrance, dries 4 metres.

Many fish cages are anchored off the east side of Ardheslaig, and the inlet may now be used by work boats. Steel stakes, dangerous to inflatable dinghies, were found at the north end of the beach some years ago.

Upper Loch Torridon

A clean passage 2 cables wide leads from the northeast side of Loch Shieldaig to Upper Loch Torridon which is generally free from dangers apart from detached drying rocks in two places 1¼ cables off the south shore.

Occasional anchorages may be found in most of the inlets around the shore, depending on wind direction, but some are occupied by fish cages.

The upper loch is very squally if there is any wind.

Camas Doire Aonar on the southwest shore is full of small-boat moorings, but good shelter and holding are found off the entrance in a strong southwest wind.

Inverbain Islands, 1 mile west of Shieldaig Island, have a basin on their south side which might be worth investigating.

A rock which dries 1·2 metres lies ½ cable west of the northwest island, and drying rocks lie in the middle of the passage south of that island but an apparently clear channel lies between the rocks and the island.

There is a sheltered anchorage between the

Anchorages

Camas an Lein, on the east side of the peninsula which separates Loch Shieldaig from the upper loch, provides good shelter in westerly winds.

A rock dries 2·4 metres 1 cable off the south point of the bay.

Ob a' Bhraighe on the north shore NNE of Rubh' a' Ghiubhais, ¾ mile ENE of the narrows, has a rock which dries 1·5 metres ½ cable off the west side of the entrance.

Bay west of Rubh na Feola (57°32'N 05°37'N). Reefs on either side extend ½ cable from point on west side and from an equivalent location due east of that point.

Ob Gorm Beag has 3 rows of floats across it with a gap at alternate ends of each row, and a mooring for a fishing boat at the head.

Ob Gorm Mor has only two rows of floats, and there is more space to anchor.

At the ***head of the loch***, the best anchorage is on the south side close to the southwest shore, between a jetty at Eilean Chasgaig ¼ mile northwest of the hotel and Rubha an t-Salainn, a wooded rocky promontory 3 cables northwest of it. Hotel nearby.

Torridon village, on the north side of the head of the loch, has a shop and a post office.

Anchor in quiet weather northwest of the head of a promontory which extends from the east shore.

Loch Gairloch

Charts
2528 (1:15,000), *2210* (1:50,000)
OS map *19*

Tides
Constant −0020 Ullapool (−0440 Dover)

Height in metres

MHWS	MHWN	MTL	MLWN	MLWS
5·2	4·0	3·0	1·8	0·6

Dangers and marks
The loch is clean except within the inlets of the south shore and between Eilean Horrisdale and Loch Shieldaig.

Glas Eilean, towards the head of the loch, has a light beacon at its centre.

Longa Island lies ½ mile from the north point of the entrance; in Caolas Beag, the channel between Longa and the mainland, the shore dries for 2 cables.

Lights
Glas Eilean Fl.WRG.6s9m6-4M
Gairloch Pier head Q.R.9m
Glas Eilean light beacon shows white towards the entrance clear of danger and towards Loch Shieldaig and the approach to Gairloch Pier.

Badachro (Caolas Bad a' Chrotha)
57°42'N 5°43'W

A well-sheltered inlet, easy to approach but quite fully occupied by fishing boats and local yachts.

Dangers and marks
On the west side of the channel an above-water rock stands at the east end of a drying reef leaving a passage ½ cable wide between the rock and Eilean

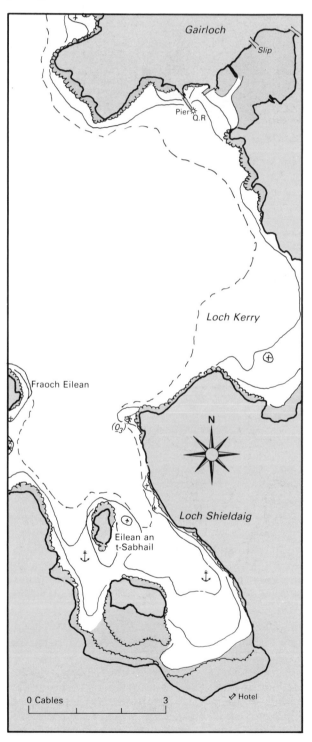

Gairloch Pier and Loch Shieldaig

Badachro from the head of the slip.

Horrisdale; beware also of the drying reef to the east of the visible rock.

A submerged rock lies ½ cable SSE of the above-water rock at a depth of 0·9 metres.

A rock which dries 3·7 metres on the southeast side of the fairway south of two tidal islets is marked by a perch.

The head of the inlet dries off ¼ mile.

The fairway is lined with moorings on either side.

The hotel has two visitors' moorings.

A stone jetty and slipway stand on the west side of the mouth of a river which runs out on the south shore.

The bed of the river effectively dries and the current is strong, especially after rain but, with care,

a yacht can go alongside after half flood to take on water from a hose.

A post stands on the west side of the slip and, when the foot of the post is covered, there is 2·4 metres depth at the east side of the slip.

If Badachro is too crowded, space can be found to anchor in *The Bird's Nest*, SSE of Eilean Horrisdale, (see below) The passage south of Eilean Horrisdale, although tortuous, can be negotiated with care.

Supplies

Shop, telephone, hotel, baths at hotel, the hotel, water at slip, *Calor Gas*, chandlery, diesel from chandlery.

Other anchorages

The Bird's Nest, 57°41'·5N 5°41'W or east of Horrisdale Island, inshore of Sgeir Dubh Bheag.

Loch Shieldaig, 57°41'·5N 5°41'W, in the southeast corner of Loch Gairloch, is occupied by moorings, many of them belonging to east-coast fishing boats and often not used during the summer.

If there is no space in the main part of the loch, anchor SSW of Eilean an t-Sabhail or in Camas na h-Airighe, southwest of Fraoch Eilean.

A rock, which dries 0·3 metres, lies ¼ cable off the east point of the entrance to Loch Shieldaig.

Submerged rocks lie up to ¾ cable southwest of Fraoch Eilean, and a rock 1 cable south of the island dries 1·1 metres.

Drying rocks lie less than a cable off the east side of Eilean Horrisdale but shelter may be found clear of them.

Loch Kerry is partly occupied by fish cages and a submerged rock lies in the middle of the bay 1 cable from the southwest shore.

Flowerdale Bay

Gairloch Pier, 57°42'·6N 5°41'W, is used by fishing boats, and dues are charged even to go alongside for water.

The river mouth dries off 2 cables and yachts should go no further in than a line joining the head of the east pier and the promontory on the south side of the river.

Landing at steps at old stone pier.

Supplies

Shop, post office, telephone, hotel, bank, petrol at garage and diesel at pier. Water by hose at pier, *Calor Gas* and mechanical repairs – ask at garage. Launching slip, sailing club, chandlery.

Showers and meals at the Old Inn.

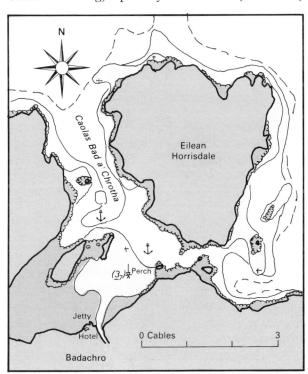

Badachro

Loch Shieldaig, Gairloch

East shore of Raasay

Charts

2498, 2534 (1:25,000), *2209* (1:50,000)
OS maps *24, 32*
OS Outdoor Leisure Map – *The Cuillin and Torridon Hills* (1:25,000) provides more detail of the southwest side of the Inner Sound

Occasional anchorage (Inner Sound)

Hallaig: an open bay on the east side of Raasay, 2 miles north of Eyre Point light beacon, exposed N–NE, with a shingle beach at the head, and a shingle spit extending north from Rudha na Leac at the east side of the bay. An occasional anchorage with possibilities for scrambling ashore.

Broadford Bay

Tides

In Caolas Pabay, the northeast-going stream begins +0550 Ullapool (+0130 Dover)

The southwest-going stream begins −0010 Ullapool (−0430 Dover) at a spring rate of 1 knot

Dangers and marks

The Skye shore is fringed with drying reefs and rocks, in places extending 3½ cables from the shore; the most extensive are south of Pabay.

Drying rocks extend ½ mile SSW of Pabay to Sgeir Ghobhlach on which stands an iron beacon 9 metres high with a cage topmark.

Submerged rocks lie 1½ cables southwest of the beacon.

An Admiralty mooring buoy (Fl.Y.5s) lies 070° about ½mile from the head of Corry Pier.

Directions

From Kyle Akin pass north of both of the red buoys west of the (disused) lighthouse and from the second buoy (*Bow Rock*) steer for Sgeir Ghobhlach beacon; when the east side of Pabay is abeam, steer for the southwest corner of Broadford Bay.

Anchorages

In Broadford Bay, a convenient anchorage is off Corry Pier on the west side of the bay, but a drying rock lies about ½ cable south of the head of the pier.

It may be possible to lie at the south side of the pier and go ashore for stores, but all space may be taken by fishing boats and some crew should stay aboard in case it is necessary to move.

It may be possible to lie at the drying pier on the south side of the bay near high water.
See colour photo facing page 106

Supplies at Broadford

Shops, post office, telephone, hotel, petrol and diesel at garage. Laundrette at Broadford Hotel (check first), 24-hour fuel, shopping and laundrette at Sutherland's garage. Dentist and hospital.

Port nam Murrach (see page 16) *Opposite* Camas Darrach, at the tip of the Sleat Peninsula (see page 63)

Below Soay Harbour from east, well sheltered by the Skye shore opposite (see page 46)

Isleornsay from west (see page 64)

Loch Nevis Narrows with Tarbert Bay at lower right

Caolas Scalpay with the shallow rocky channel showing clearly under
water (see page 91)

Loch Torridon, looking east over the Ardheslaig Peninsula to
Loch Sheildag (see page 85)

Acarsaid Mor, Rona (see page 98)

Eilean Fladday (see page 96)

VI. Sound of Raasay

Caolas Scalpay

See colour photo between pages 90 and 91.

Tides

The east-going stream begins +0550 Ullapool (+0130 Dover)

The west-going stream begins −0010 Ullapool (−0430 Dover), at a spring rate of 1 knot

Directions

From *Kyle Akin*, approach as for Broadford and continue on that course until ¼ mile beyond a point where the beacon is abeam.

Alternatively, pass north of Pabay, but note that drying reefs extend 3 cables north and northwest of the island.

In Caolas Scalpay, drying reefs extend 1 cable from Scalpay and a shingle bank extends north from Skye, with a depth of only 0·1 metres in the narrowest part between them.

A leading line to help in finding the channel is the school house at Dunan, a white building on the Skye shore, west of the narrows, under the peak of An Coileach which is beyond, and to the right of, the summit of Am Meall, 291°, as shown in the photo.

Anchorage

As convenient, either east or west of the narrows. Either may be squally.

Note Sgeir Stapaig, which dries, a cable off the Scalpay shore east of the narrows.

Fish cages are moored off both shores.

At night

The cages off the south shore are marked by Q.Y light buoys.

An Goileach

Caolas Scalpay leading line.

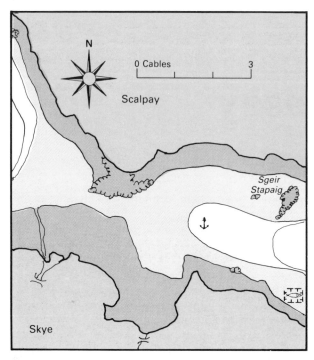

Caolas Scalpay

Loch Ainort

57°17'N 6°02'W

A wild and rather featureless loch surrounded by high hills.

Anchor either at Luib on the southeast side of the loch, in a slight indentation off the mouth of a valley, or in the south or west corners of the head of the loch.

Caol Mor and Sound of Raasay

57°20'N 6°05'W

Charts

2534, 2498 (1:25,000) for approach, *2209* (1:50,000)
OS map *24*

Tides

In Caol Mor, the spring rate is 1 knot; in Linne Crowlin, southwest of Crowlin Islands it is ½ knot, and, between Scalpay and Longay, 2 knots.

The southeast and east-going stream begins +0605 Ullapool (+0145 Dover)

The northwest and west-going stream begins +0005 Ullapool (−0415 Dover)

Constant −0025 Ullapool (−0445 Dover)

Height in metres

MHWS	MHWN	MTL	MLWN	MLWS
5·3	3·7	2·9	1·9	0·7

Dangers and marks in the approach to Caol Mor from southeast

Longay, ENE of Scalpay, has drying reefs ¾ cable southwest and 1½ cables northwest of it.

Sgeir Dhearg, an islet 8 metres high surrounded by reefs lies ¾ mile northwest of Scalpay.

Gulnare Rock which dries, halfway between Sgeir Dhearg and Scalpay, is marked on its south side by a green conical buoy.

Sgeir Thraid, a reef drying 4 metres 6 cables WNW of Sgeir Dhearg, is marked by a red iron beacon with a cage topmark.

Pass either southwest or northeast of these rocks as convenient with due care.

Light

A light beacon Fl.WR.3s5m9/6M stands at Eyre Point on the northeast side of Caol Mor showing red over the dangers described above, and white elsewhere.

Loch Sligachan

57°19'N 6°07'W

Like Loch Ainort, a wild and mountainous loch subject to squalls but convenient for an expedition to the Red Cuillins.

Tides

The spring rate in the entrance is 1½ knots.

The in-going stream begins +0605 Ullapool (+0145 Dover)

The out-going stream begins −0015 Ullapool (−0435 Dover)

Dangers and marks

The entrance is partly blocked by An Corran, a drying spit on the north side. A ferry to Raasay operates from a slip on the south shore of the loch.

A shoal extends 4 cables from the south shore outside the entrance to Bo Sligachan, over which the depth is 0·4 metres.

Sconser Lodge, a stone house on the shore east of the entrance with a few trees around it, in line with the summit of Sgurr Mhairi, the highest hill on the south side of the loch, 215°, leads WNW of the shoals to the entrance. 1 cable from the shore turn west and then WNW to pass south of An Corran which shows pale below the water.

A light Q.R. shows from the ferry slip.

Anchorages

Peinchorran, within the entrance on the north side.

Sgeir Dhubh 0·6 metre high lies a cable off the northeast side of the bay and disused underwater cables (marked by rusty red cable beacons) lie across the loch ½ cable further west from a ruined slip on the north shore.

Anchor to the west of the ruined slip.

Sgurr Mhairi

Loch Sligachan approach.

Photo: Jean Lawrence

Loch Sligachan from southwest, with the spit An Corran at the
left-hand side and shoals showing under water

The head of the loch dries for more than ½ mile and banks on either side dry for more than a cable in places.

Anchor towards the head of the loch, in a depth of not less than 5 metres as the bottom rises abruptly.

Sligachan Inn is famous as a climbers' hostelry.

Raasay Narrows

57°20'·5N 6°05'W

Tides

The south-going stream begins −0605 Ullapool (+0200 Dover)

The north-going stream begins −0040 Ullapool (−0500 Dover)

Constant −0025 Ullapool (−0445 Dover)

Height in metres

MHWS	MHWN	MTL	MLWN	MLWS
5·3	3·7	2·9	1·9	0·7

Dangers and marks

(In sequence from south to north)
The passage is ½ mile wide between An Aird on Skye and Eilean Aird nan Gobhar, southwest of Ardhuish on Raasay, northeast of An Aird.

Suisnish Pier stands at the southwest point of Raasay.

Rainy Rocks, drying 1·1 metres, lie 1 cable east of the east point of An Aird.

Penfold Rock red can buoy 2 cables northeast of An Aird, and *Jackal Rock* green conical buoy 6 cables east of An Aird, both mark rocks at a depth of 2·9 metres.

McMillan's Rock, 4 cables north of An Aird at a depth of 0·4 metre, is marked on its west side by a green conical light buoy.

A submerged rock lies a cable west of Eilean Aird nan Gobhar at a depth of 1·3 metres.

Sgeir Chnapach, 3 metres high, lies 1¼ miles north of Ardhuish, 3 cables from Raasay, with drying rocks inshore of it.

Direction

Pass northeast of *Penfold Rock* buoy to keep clear of Rainy Rocks.

McMillan's Rock light buoy should be passed on its west side, or not less than a cable to the east.

Lights

Eyre Point light beacon Fl.WR.3s5m6/9M shows
   red over dangers in approach from east.
Suisnish Point pier head 2F.G(vert)
McMillan's Rock light buoy Fl(2)G.12s

At night

From east keep north of the red sector of Eyre Point light. In Caol Mor this light is obscured north of 063° but a direct course between Suisnish Pier and

the west side of *McMillan's Rock* buoy clears all dangers.

There are no lights further north in the Sound of Raasay, but a mid-channel course can be estimated until Portree Harbour opens up. Look out for Sgeir Cnapach, described above.

Minor anchorages

Balmeanach Bay, 57°20'N 6°06'W, southwest of An Aird.

Two underwater power cables cross to Raasay from a point marked by a pole 2 cables west of the southwest point of An Aird, and part of the bay is taken up by fish cages.

Holding has been found to be good.

Camas a' Mhor-bheoil, 57°20'·5N 6°06'·5W, lies west of the north point of An Aird.

Sgeir Dhubh, 3 metres high, lies 3½ cables northwest of the north point of An Aird, and a rock at the 2-metre contour ¼ mile from the head of the bay dries 0·8 metre.

Northerly swell sets into the bay.

Churchton Bay, Raasay, 57°21'N 6°05'W, southeast of Ardhuish.

Perch Rocks, drying 2·9 metres lie more than a cable southwest from a promontory in front of Raasay House; the outer rock is marked by an iron perch.

Anchor either side of the rocks. The southeast side of the bay is foul with submerged rocks more than a cable offshore.

Visitors' moorings (blue buoys) are laid off the hotel ESE of Perch Rocks. Exposed SW.

Portree

57°25'N 6°11'W

Westerly winds funnel fiercely out of Portree Harbour and down the sides of the hills making it difficult for a sailing boat to approach in these conditions.

Tides

Constant −0025 Ullapool (−0445 Dover)

Height in metres

MHWS	MHWN	MTL	MLWN	MLWS
5·3	3·7	2·9	1·9	0·7

Dangers and marks

Sgeir Mhor, a reef partly above water which extends a cable from a promontory on the north shore, ½ mile east of Portree Pier, is marked by a green conical light buoy.

Fish cages, together with a submerged rock, lie up to a cable off shore northeast of Sgeir Mhor.

A yellow conical light buoy about 1½ cables SSE of the pier, lies in 3 metres about a cable from the LW mark at the mouth of Loch Portree, the whole of which dries.

Portree from northeast

Photo: Mike Balmforth

Portree pier from north at low water

Lights

Sgeir Mhor light buoy Fl.G 5s
Yellow light buoy Fl.Y 5s
A light at the pier head, 2F.R(vert)6m4M, is only
shown occasionally

Anchorages

Much of the area northeast of the pier dries; a large
area is occupied by moorings, marked by buoys, and
anchoring there should be avoided.

The anchorage east of the pier in 7–10 metres is
soft mud with not very good holding.

There are visitors' moorings off the north shore
but these may be found untenable in a southerly
wind owing to the fetch from Loch Portree.

The north side of the pier and stone slip dries almost
completely at springs but a yacht may be able to go
alongside temporarily at a suitable rise of tide; the
sea level may be raised deceptively by the wind and
there are small underwater obstructions at the slip.
Dues are charged, although not for a brief visit, and
crew should remain on board at all times to shift
berth if necessary. It may be possible to remain at
the pier overnight on Friday and Saturday nights.

Camas Ban, east of Vriskaig Point, is subject to
severe downdraughts in southerly winds.

These downdraughts are known locally as
'whirlies' and, anywhere along the east side of
Trotternish in strong southerlies, they can be seen
spinning over the surface and sucking up a rotating
cloud of spray.

Admiralty vessels sometimes use this anchorage
but are unlikely to lie as far inshore as a yacht would
anchor.

Supplies

Shops (supermarket, Dunvegan Road), post office,
telephone, hotels, swimming pool (limited opening
to public), showers at the Independent Hostel in
The Square.

Diesel, only in multiples of 10 gallons, from BP
depot on the pier. Water from hose at pier. Petrol
and diesel, *Calor Gas*, also mechanical repairs, at
West End Garage (½ mile on Dunvegan Road).

Chandlery and hardware: North Skye Fishermen's
Association on the pier, Bow and Stern and
JansVans are both at Dunvegan Road.

Fladday Harbour

57°28'·5N 6°01'·3W
See colour photo facing page 91.

Southeast of Fladday Island on the west side of the
north end of Raasay.

Charts

2209 (2210), (1:50,000)
OS map 24

Tides

Constant −0025 Ullapool (−0445 Dover)

Fladday Harbour.

Sound of Raasay

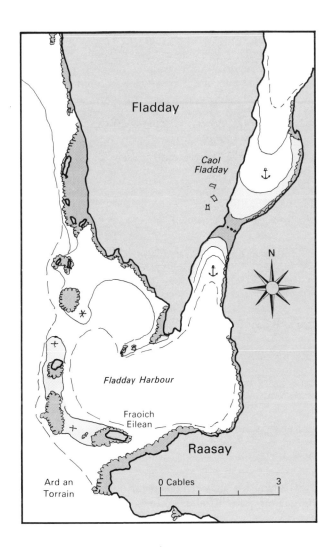

Height in metres

MHWS	MHWN	MTL	MLWN	MLWS
5·3	3·7	2·9	1·9	0·7

Dangers and marks

Griana-sgeir, 7 metres high, and a line of rocks lie between ¼ and ½ mile west of Fladday.

Bo Leachan, south of Griana-sgeir, is cleared by keeping the west tangent of Rona open west of Griana-sgeir 018°.

Bo na Currachie, north of Griana-sgeir, is cleared by keeping the west tangent of Raasay open west of Griana-sgeir 201°.

At Manish Point, the south point of Loch Arnish, drying reefs extend more than a cable northwest.

The southwest side of the bay is enclosed by islets and drying rocks which, depending on the light, may be very difficult to distinguish; a few cottages on the shore of Loch Arnish may help to identify the way in.

Two cottages on Fladday show up well if there is any afternoon sunshine.

Directions

The entrance is about 60 metres wide between Ard an Torrain on Raasay and Fraoich Eilean ½ cable northwest of it, which must be identified before proceeding.

Drying reefs are said to extend part of the way across the passage from Ard an Torrain, but the depth in the northwest half of the passage is at least 6 metres.

After passing Fraoich Eilean head for the inlet between Fladday and Raasay.

Detached drying rocks, WSW of the south point of Fladday, shown on the plan in the previous *Pilot*, apparently do not exist, but the whole area should be treated with caution as there is no detailed survey.

The inlet is blocked ¼ mile from its mouth by boulders and a stone causeway which all dry at low water; take care not to go too far in. It has been noted that this inlet is occupied by a permanently moored barge or work-boat.

The bottom appears to be stony with weed, but there is some clear sand under the cliffs of Fladday.

Caol Fladda (Fladday North Harbour) is the north part of the inlet between Fladday and Raasay. It is full of kelp and the holding is said to be poor.

Bo na Faochag at a depth of 1·8 metres lies 3½ cables north of Fladday; the summit of Beinn na h-Iolaire, open east of Fladday 156°, leads 1½ cables east of Bo na Faochag.

Fladday Harbour approach, from northeast. A yacht is in the passage between Ard an Torrain, on the extreme left, and Fraoich Eilean. The south point of Fladday is at the right.

Caol Rona

Waypoint
East end 57°30'·3N 5°58'·5W
West end 57°31'·2N 6°00'W

Charts
2479 (1:18,000)
OS map 24

Tides

The southeast-going stream begins +0505 Ullapool (+0045 Dover)

The northwest-going stream begins −0055 Ullapool (−0515 Dover)

The spring rate is at least 2 knots. The northwest-going stream sets towards Eilean Seamraig.

Dangers and marks

Eilean an Fhraoich stands in the middle of the channel with a beacon No. 4 on its southwest side.

Eilean Seamraig on the northeast side of the channel is separated from Garbh Eilean by a channel obstructed by rocks. Garbh Eilean is a tidal islet joined to Rona by a stony isthmus.

A submerged rock lies ½ cable southwest of Eilean an Fhraoich at a depth of 0·4 metres and a drying reef extends ½ cable northwest.

No. 5 beacon stands on Rubha Ard Ghlaisen on Raasay, nearly a mile SSE of Eilean an Fhraoich.

A light beacon, No. 8, an orange and white triangle, stands on the southeast point of Garbh Eilean.

Eilean an Fhraoich can be passed on either side.

Lights

Rona lighthouse Fl.12s69m19M obscured 358°-050°
Ru na Lachan light beacon Oc.WR.8s21m10M, ¾ mile north of the Range Control building, shows red towards Caol Rona
Light beacon No. 8 Fl.3s8m5M

Anchorage – Garbh Eilean

On the northeast side of the Kyle, at the northwest end of Garbh Eilean, a straightforward inlet with a landing place and rough track on the north side, approximately opposite the west end of Garbh Eilean. A drying reef extends ½ cable from the west end of Garbh Eilean.

Acairseid Mhor, Rona

Waypoint 57°31'·8N 6°00'W
See colour photo facing page 91.

A popular anchorage on the west side of Rona. Difficult to identify, as Eilean Garbh in the entrance merges with the background, but a white arrow is painted on the south side of the island to help identification.

Survey information for Acarseid Mor seems to be under a spell and drying heights of rocks shown on the plan are only approximate, or even positively doubtful. In spite of the area being frequently visited by many yachts, new rocks are still being discovered. Even the Hydrographic Office is affected, as a previous edition of the large-scale BA chart showed Sgeir na h'Acarseid as drying 5·3 metres. Further observations will be gratefully received.

Charts
2479 (1:18,000)
OS map *24*

Tides
Constant −0025 Ullapool (−0445 Dover)

Height in metres

MHWS	MHWN	MTL	MLWN	MLWS
5·3	3·7	2·9	1·9	0·7

Directions

Approach southeast of Eilean Garbh and pass between Sgeir na h'Acarseid and the promontory close southeast of it. If the rock is covered, pass the promontory about 10 metres off on a line with the southeast tangent of Eilean Garbh astern; the rock shows pale below the water. Some experienced skippers prefer to pass west and north of Sgeir na h'Acarseid when it is covered.

Steer for Eilean na h'Acarseid and, when within about a cable of it, alter course towards the cottage to pass west of the islet.

A rock at a depth of 1·2 metres was discovered the hard way some years ago, ½ cable NNW of Eilean na h'Acarseid.

In the passage north of Eilean Garbh there are no reference points, but rocks on either side of the passage are usually marked by swell breaking on them.

Anchorage

Anchor northwest or northeast of Eilean na h'Acarseid clear of drying reefs as shown.

Holding is poor in places, consisting of soft black mud, well ploughed by yachts' anchors.

Two mooring buoys are laid in the inner part of the harbour.

There is said to be space to anchor west of the reef west of the jetty.

The anchorage formerly shown just east of the drying rock in the entrance has a rocky bottom, and submerged rocks lie close enough to the surface to embarrass a yacht.

The jetty was not convenient for landing from a small boat at low tide, but the proprietors were planning to install a floating pontoon during the winter of 1996/97. There are cleared landing places in most of the bays round the shore.

Acairseid Mhor, Rona from the head of the inlet.

Acairseid Mhor, Rona

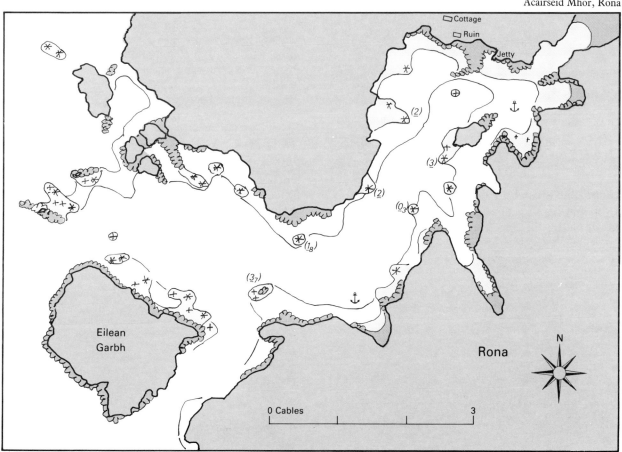

Toilets and showers have been provided near the jetty.

VHF is watched on Ch 12 – call sign *Rona Lodge*.

Loch a' Bhraige

Waypoint 57°35'N 6°59'W

Chart

2534 (1:7,500)

This inlet is used by the Admiralty and is elaborately marked and lit, providing a harbour, if needed, when coming from the north of Skye after dark but it has little other attraction for a yacht.

Directions

Sgeir Shuas is a group of islets on the north side of the entrance, on one of which is a light beacon.

A drying rock lies ¾ cable southwest of the north point of the loch, otherwise it is clean to near the head of the inlet where a reef, partly above water, with light beacon No. 9 on it, extends 1½ cables northwest from the shore.

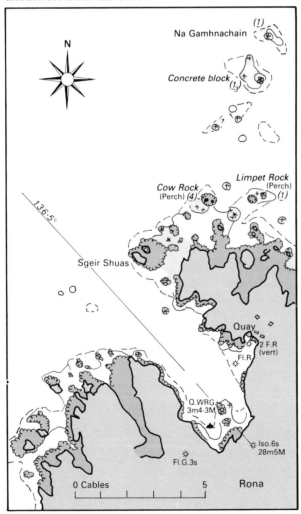

Loch a' Bhraige

The inlet in the northeast corner, where there is a piled quay with rubber fendering, gives good shelter. Admiralty vessels often lie at the quay overnight.

Pass either side of the detached light beacon and anchor in the northeast inlet clear of the approach to the quay.

Alternative anchorages are either side of the reef on which beacon No. 9 stands; a mooring buoy is laid south of the reef.

Lights

Rona lighthouse Fl.12s69m19M obscd 358°- 050°
Sgeir Shuas light beacon Fl.R.2s6m3M
No. 9 light beacon Q.WRG.3m4-3M
No. 10 light beacon Iso.6s28m5M
Detached light beacon off NE inlet Fl.R.5s4m3M
Quay, southwest corner 2F.R(vert)
No. 1 light beacon Fl.G.3s91m3M

At night

Light beacons No. 9 and No. 10 in line lead into the loch 136·5°.

Passage at the North end of Rona

Dangers and marks

Rocks, submerged and drying, extend 8 cables north of Rona to Na Gamhnachain which dries 1 metre.

A rock 1½ cables south of Na Gamhnachain has a concrete block built up on it which dries 1·3 metres.

Several submerged rocks lie between Na Gamhnachain and Rona.

Cow Rock, 4 metres high, 2 cables north of the northwest point of Rona, and Limpet Rock, 1 metre high and 2 cables further east, both have perches on them.

A submerged rock at a depth of 1·8 metres lies ½ cable north of a direct line between these two rocks, apart from which the nearest charted hazard is a submerged rock 2 cables north of Cow Rock. An inshore passage north of these rocks may be taken in clear settled weather.

Northeast Skye

Rubha na h-Aiseig is the northeast point, and Rubha Hunish the northwest point of Trotternish, the north peninsula of Skye.

Eilean Trodday, a grassy flat-topped island, with a light beacon on its centre, lies nearly a mile north of Rubha na h-Aiseig.

The west side of Skye is described in Chapter III.

Charts

2210 (1:50,000)
OS map *23*

Tides

Tidal streams round the north end of Skye follow the coast with eddies in the bays between headlands.

Staffin Bay from southeast

Heavy overfalls occur between Rubha na h-Aiseig and Staffin Bay.

In the passage between Rubha na h-Aiseig on Skye and Eilean Trodday the spring rate is 2½ knots.

The east-going stream begins −0350 Ullapool (+0415 Dover)

The west-going stream begins +0235 Ullapool (−0145 Dover)

Off Rubha Hunish the spring rate is 2½ knots.

The northeast-going stream begins −0405 Ullapool (+0400 Dover)

The southwest-going stream begins +0220 Ullapool (−0200 Dover)

Lights
Eilean Trodday Fl(2)WRG.10s49m12-9M
Rona Fl.12s69m19M 358°-obscd-050°

Minor anchorages
Staffin Bay, 57°38'·5N 6°13'W, is a clean, open bay exposed northeast and subject to squalls in westerly winds. Eilean Floddigarry provides some shelter from the north.

Clach nan Ramh, 2 cables off Skye, 7 cables NNW of Eilean Flodigarry, north of Staffin Bay, dries 3·8 metres. If approaching or leaving by the passage between Skye and Eilean Flodigarry, when beyond the north end of Flodigarry keep Staffin Island hidden behind Eilean Flodigarry, 153°, to clear this rock.

Anchor either on the east side of the bay or in its southwest corner.

The passage between Staffin Island and Skye is blocked by rocks.

A shop and restaurant stand on the main road ½ mile from Quiraing Lodge, the large house at the mouth of a burn on the south side of the bay.

Kilmaluag Bay, 57°41'·5N 6°18'W, a small inlet ¾ mile south of Rubha na h-Aiseig, is convenient for waiting for suitable conditions for a passage beyond the north end of Skye or as an overnight anchorage in settled weather, although the bottom is stony in places and the anchor chain may grumble.

A drying reef extends more than 1½ cables from the south point of the entrance. The bay is subject to fierce squalls in strong westerly winds.

VII. Northwest mainland

Passage notes – Rubha Reidh to Loch Inchard

Waypoint 2 miles west of Rubha Reidh 51°57'·6N 5°52'W

Waypoint 1 mile NW of Point of Stoer 57°16'·5N 5°25'W

The 40 miles of coast from Rubha Reidh to Loch Inchard is deeply indented, consisting of great bays between impressive headlands, with almost no continuous length of coastline facing seaward.

Two of the headlands, Rubha Reidh and Point of Stoer, are notorious for heavy seas, caused mainly by their exposure and the strength of the tidal streams around them.

Seas around these headlands are particularly dangerous with wind against tide and they should be given a berth of several miles if it is necessary to pass them under such conditions.

Charts

1794, 1785 (1:100,000)
OS maps *19, 15, 9*

Tides at Rubha Reidh

The northeast-going stream begins −0335 Ullapool (+0430 Dover)

The southwest-going stream begins +0305 Ullapool (−0115 Dover)

The spring rate of these streams is 3 knots. There may be eddies inshore on the downstream side of the point.

At Rubha Coigeach and Point of Stoer:

The north-going stream begins −0250 Ullapool (+0515 Dover)

The south-going stream begins +0420 Ullapool (HW Dover)

The spring rate of these streams is 2½ knots.

Dangers and marks

Rubha Reidh (57°52'N 5°48'W) is marked by a white lighthouse 25 metres in height, and a conspicuous radio mast stands on a hill 1½ miles southeast of the point.

Point of Stoer is a bold headland with a stack, the Old Man of Stoer, 56 metres in height, on its northwest side, which shows very distinctly from northeast. Stoerhead lighthouse, a white tower 14 metres in height stands on a cliff 1¾ miles SSW of the point.

Lights

Rubha Reidh Fl(4)15s37m24M
Soyea Island (Loch Inver) Fl(2)10s34m6M
Stoerhead Fl.15s59m24M
Rubha na Leacaig (Loch Inchard) Fl(2)10s30m8M
Tiumpan Head (Lewis) Fl(2)15s55m25M
Cape Wrath lighthouse Fl(4)30s122m24M is obscured east of 025°

At night, in clear moderate weather, these lights will be sufficient for a passage along the coast.

Radiobeacons

Stornoway Aero 669·5kHz *SAY* (···/·−/−·−−) 60M
    58°12'·86N 6°19'·49W (non-A2A)
Butt of Lewis 289kHz *BL* (−···/·−··) 70M
    58°30'·93N 6°15'·72W

Shelter

Loch Torridon, Gairloch, Isle of Ewe in Loch Ewe, Summer Isles, Loch Inver, various lochs on the south side of Eddrachillis Bay, Loch Laxford, Kinlochbervie; all provide some shelter during a passage along the coast.

Loch Ewe

57°51'N 5°40'W

Charts

2509 (1:25,000) approach only, *3146* (1:12,500)
OS map *19*

Tides

Off the entrance, tidal streams run at up to 2½ knots.

The NNE-going stream begins −0335 Ullapool (+0430 Dover)

The SSW-going stream begins +0305 Ullapool (−0115 Dover)

Within the loch, streams turn at HW and LW and may reach 1 knot in narrower passages.

Constant −0010 Ullapool (−0430 Dover)

Height in metres

MHWS	MHWN	MTL	MLWN	MLWS
5·1	3·8	2·9	2·0	0·7

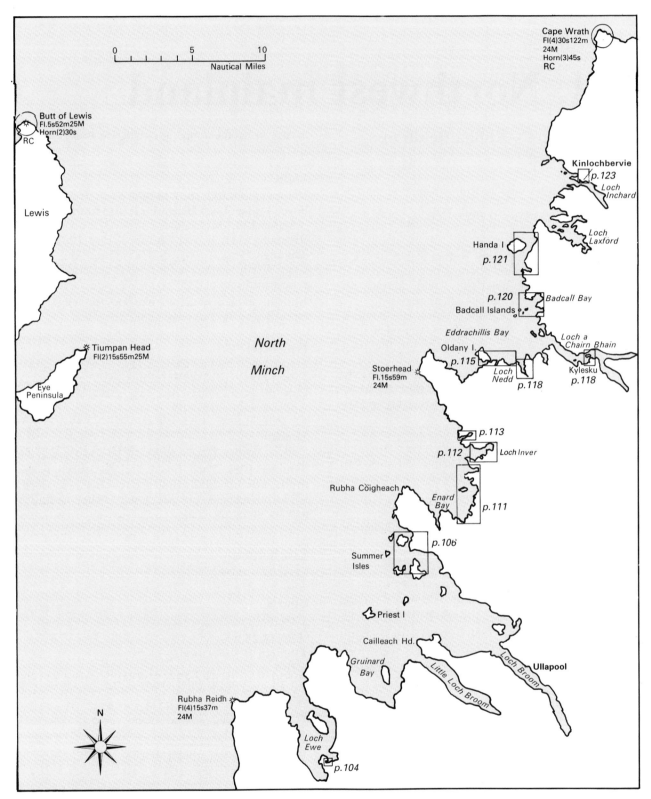

0   5   10
Nautical Miles

Cape Wrath
Fl(4)30s122m
24M
Horn(3)45s
RC

Butt of Lewis
Fl.5s52m25M
Horn(2)30s
RC

Lewis

Kinlochbervie
p.123
Loch Inchard

Loch Laxford

Handa I
p.121

Loch a Chairn Bhain

p.120
Badcall Islands
Badcall Bay

Eddrachillis Bay

North Minch

Tiumpan Head
Fl(2)15s55m25M

Oldany I.
p.115
Loch Nedd
p.118
Kylesku
p.118

Eye Peninsula

Stoerhead
Fl.15s59m
24M

p.113
p.112
Loch Inver

Rubha Còigheach
Enard Bay
p.111

p.106

Summer Isles

Priest I

Cailleach Hd.

Gruinard Bay

Little Loch Broom

Loch Broom
Ullapool

Rubha Reidh
Fl(4)15s37m
24M

N

Loch Ewe
p.104

Directions

The entrance lies 4 miles east of Rubha Reidh and has no hidden dangers.

Fairway buoy (RW) and No. 1 green conical light buoy are in the fairway.

Isle of Ewe, 2 miles long, is near the east shore of the loch, and Sgeir an Araig, 12 metres high, is ½ mile northwest of Isle of Ewe.

The passage round the south end of Isle of Ewe is marked by three red can light buoys.

A NATO fuelling jetty is on the mainland ESE of the Isle of Ewe.

Greenstone Point, 3½ miles NNE of the entrance to Loch Ewe, produces heavy seas with wind against tide.

Lights

Fairway light buoy LFl.10s

No. 1 light buoy Fl(3)G.10s

Red light buoys east of Ewe Island:
D (south) Fl(2)R.10s
E (middle) Fl.R.2s
F (north) Fl(4)R.10s

NATO fuelling jetty and dolphins north and south each Fl.G.4s

Anchorages

Several bays on the west side of the loch provide an occasional overnight anchorage to save going further up the loch.

Acairseid nan Uamh, 1 mile SSW of the Fairway buoy, has been found satisfactory in settled weather.

Acairseid Mhor, 57°50'·6N 5°38'W, sometimes known as Camas Angus, on the east side of the north end of Isle of Ewe, is clean apart from a drying reef on its south side and has been found to give good shelter and holding in gales between south and northwest.

A mooring and small fish cages lie in the mouth of the bay.

Aultbea, 57°50'·3N 5°3'·5W, on the east side of the sound is partly sheltered by Aird Point on which there is a stone pier which dries alongside, with a decaying timber-piled pier head.

Much of the bay inshore of the pier dries or is shoal, with moorings for inshore fishing boats.

Anchor off a hotel on the east shore, or close east of the pier for some protection from northwest.

In west or southwest winds, Acairseid Mhor gives better shelter.

Supplies

Shop (Bridgend Stores, chart agent and *Calor Gas*), butcher ¼ mile. Post office, telephone, hotels, water tap at pier. Petrol (but not diesel) at Forbes Garage, which can help with mechanical and electrical repairs in an emergency.

Loch Thurnaig, 57°47'·5N 5°35'W, 2 miles south of Isle of Ewe.

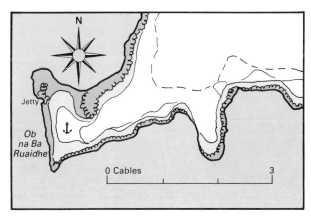

Loch Thurnaig

The bottom is soft mud with some rock, but shelter may be found in Ob na Ba Ruaidhe in the southwest corner behind a drying reef which extends from the north side of the entrance to this bay.

The bottom is partly rocky and partly very soft mud.

Camas Glas, 57°46'·7N 5°36'·5W, is an occasional anchorage from which to visit Inverewe Gardens.

Anchor off a stone jetty on the north side of Creagan nan Cudaigean, a wooded rocky promontory on the east side of the head of the loch, ½ mile north of Poolewe and the trees mop up winds from most directions.

Good holding is found south of the promontory at Port na Cloiche Gile well offshore, but the head of the bay dries off and the depth should be checked carefully.

Poolewe, at the southwest corner of the head of the loch, provides fair shelter in southwesterly winds.

Boor Rocks, 1 mile northwest of Poolewe, stand up to 3 metres above water with drying rocks more than a cable further northwest.

Supplies

Shop, post office, telephone, hotel. Petrol, *Calor Gas* and diesel at garage (which will also help with small engineering repairs). Swimming pool.

Gruinard Bay has no regular anchorages, although there are moderate depths in places around its shore and a jetty at Laide on the southwest side of the bay. Rocks are adequately shown on chart *1794*.

Shop and post office.

Cailleach Head, at the east side of Gruinard Bay 15 miles ENE of Rubha Reidh, is marked by a 6-metre-high white light beacon at a height of 55 metres.

Little Loch Broom
57°54'N 5°22'W

Charts

2500 (1:25,000)
OS map *19*

South of Cailleach Head, Ardross Rock lies 4 cables ENE of the south point of the entrance in a depth of 0·6 metres; the loch is otherwise clean but provides little shelter and the head dries off for ½ mile.

Anchor on the south side, about 1½ miles from the head of the loch at Camusnagaul, east of a slight promontory about a mile ESE of a conspicuous fish farm.

Alternatively, in northerly winds, off the jetty at Scoraig, 1 mile within the north side of the entrance.

Supplies

Hotel, telephone at Dundonnell at head of the loch. Boat-builder at Scoraig on the north side of the entrance: C D Dawson ☎ 0185 483277.

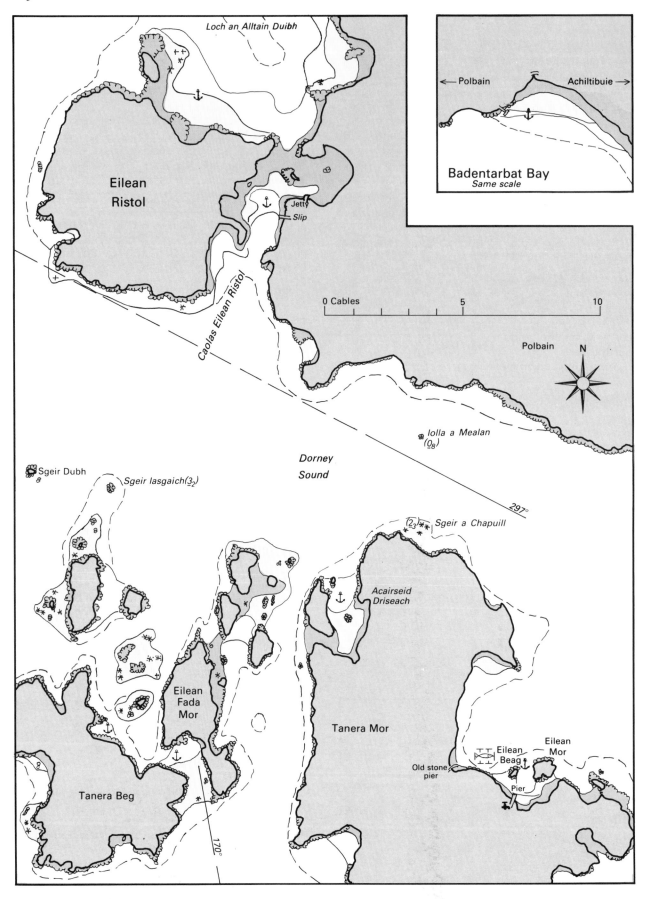

Loch an Alltain Duibh

Eilean
Ristol

Jetty
Slip

Caolas Eilean Ristol

Badentarbat Bay
Same scale

← Polbain   Achiltibuie →

0 Cables   5   10

Polbain

N

Iolla a Mealan
(O$_8$)

Dorney
Sound

297°

Sgeir Dubh

Sgeir Iasgaich(3$_2$)

(2$_3$) Sgeir a Chapuill

Acairseid
Driseach

Eilean
Fada
Mor

Tanera Mor

Tanera Beg

Eilean
Beag

Eilean
Mor

Old stone
pier

Pier

170°

Broadford Bay (see page 90). *Opposite* Kyleakin. There is, of course, no longer a vehicle ferry (see page 73).

Badcall Bay (see page 119)

Lochinver Harbour in a strong westerly wind (see page 112)

Loch Laxford, Crow Harbour, from south (see page 121)

Loch Broom

57°55'·N 5°15'W

Charts
2500 (1:25,000)
OS map *19*

Tides
Streams are weak within the loch but reach 1 knot in the narrows southeast of Ullapool.

The in-going stream begins −0555 Ullapool (+0210 Dover)

The out-going stream begins +0005 Ullapool (−0415 Dover)

Constant 0000 Ullapool (−0420 Dover)

Height in metres

MHWS	MHWN	MTL	MLWN	MLWS
5·2	3·9	3·0	2·1	0·7

Dangers and marks
A rock 1 metre high lies a cable off Leac Dhonn, 1½ miles ENE of Cailleach Head.

Rubha Cadail, 4½ miles further east, marked by a white light beacon 9 metres in height, is on the north side of the entrance to Loch Broom.

Ullapool Point (57°53'·6N 5°10'W) is on the northeast side of the loch, 2½ miles southeast of Rubha Cadail.

A red can light buoy 4 cables northwest of Ullapool Point marks shoal water at the mouth of a river.

Ullapool pier is 2 cables northeast of the point.

Ullapool
Ullapool was founded by the British Fisheries Society in 1788, and is able to provide or arrange for most services.

A large car ferry runs from Ullapool to Stornoway on Lewis. In late summer (usually after the end of the sailing season), several dozen Russian and eastern European fish-carriers, known as 'klondikers', congregate in Loch Broom and its approaches to buy fish direct from the fishing boats, generating, at times, a lot of small-boat traffic.

Lights
Cailleach Head Fl(2)12s60m9M
Rubha Cadail light beacon Fl.WRG.6s11m9-6M
Light buoy northwest of Ullapool Point Q.R
Ullapool Point Iso.R.4s8m6M
Pier 2F.R(vert)

Mooring and anchorage
Yachts can go alongside the east end, or inside the eastern arm of the pier for a short time but the depth there should be watched and some crew must stay

Ullapool pier from northeast

on board at all times to move the boat if necessary to let fishing boats in or out.

Many moorings lie east of the piers; there is space to anchor among them but yachts must keep clear of the approach to the piers; there is a lot of rubbish on the bottom and a tripping line is essential.

Some moorings are not maintained and some are in frequent use; local advice should be sought before using one.

Supplies
Shops (one of which usually opens on Sunday), post office, telephone, banks, hotels, petrol and diesel at garage, water hoses at pier. *Calor Gas* at supermarket at West Argyll Street, one block back from the pier. Chandler and chart agent also in West Argyll Street: Ullasport ☎ 01854 612621. Marine engineers and divers at the pier: Mackenzie Marine. For advice on all services, ask at Ullasport or harbourmaster ☎ 01854 612091, VHF Ch 16, 12.

Minor anchorages – Loch Broom and approaches

Loch Kanaird, 57°57'N 5°12'W, east of Isle Martin, about a mile northeast of Rubha Cadail. Entrance by the north side of the island is straightforward.

In the south entrance, drying spits extend from both sides leaving a passage ½ cable wide with no satisfactory leading line except to keep the east tangent of Isle Martin bearing 358°.

Drying rocks lie between Aird na h-Eighe, the southeast point of the bay, and Sgeir Mhor, a rock 1 metre high, about 2 cables north of the point.

There are fish cages and moorings but space will usually be found either in the bight on the east shore of Isle Martin or off Ardmair on the southeast side of the bay.

Annat Bay (Feith an Fheoir), 2 miles east of Cailleach Head. Anchor in the mouth of an inlet at the west end of the bay.

Altnaharrie, on the southwest side of the loch opposite Ullapool Point; moorings may be available overnight. Hotel and restaurant.

Loggie Bay, 57°52'N 5°07'W, on the southwest side of the loch immediately beyond the narrows 1½ miles southeast of Ullapool Point. Fish-farming rafts and moorings restrict the space.

Summer Isles

58°01'N 5°25'W

The name applies to the group of about 30 islands scattered over the approaches to Loch Broom, but only Tanera Mor and Tanera Beg on the north side have anchorages which are at all sheltered.

Priest Island, the most southwesterly of the group, has a bay on its northeast side only suitable as an occasional anchorage in settled weather. The bottom consists mainly of boulders.

This island was held for a time by French government forces during the Jacobite rising of 1745.

Charts

2501 (1:26,000)
OS map *15*

Tides

Constant −0005 Ullapool (−0425 Dover)

Height in metres

MHWS	MHWN	MTL	MLWN	MLWS
5·1	4·0	3·0	2·1	0·8

Dangers and marks

Most rocks are above water but there are drying rocks in Dorney Sound, north of Tanera Mor and Tanera Beg, in Horse Sound and south of Horse Island.

In Dorney Sound north of Tanera Mor, Iolla a Mealan, which dries 0·8 metres, is avoided by keeping the south point of Eilean Mullagrach just open south of Isle Ristol 297°.

On the south side of the sound, Sgeir Iasgaich, which dries 3·7 metres 3 cables east of Sgeir Dubh, is clear of the fairway but should be watched for.

Sgeir a Chapuill, a cable north of Tanera Mor, dries 2·3 metres.

In Horse Sound, Iolla Beg and Mary Rock are drying rocks ¼ mile off Rubha Dubh Ard at the southeast point of the sound.

They are cleared by keeping the northeast tangent of Meall nan Gabhar at the north end of Horse Island in line with Rubha Dunan, the point of the mainland to the north, and the summit of Meall an Fheadain 331°.

The north end of Stac Mhic Aonghais open south of Horse Island 283° leads south of Iolla Beg.

Iolla Mhor, 2 cables south of Horse Island, dries 3·9 metres.

Anchorages

Achiltibuie Anchor ESE of pier on the northwest side of Badentarbat Bay, but not further inshore as it is shoal.

Hotel and shops nearby; Polbain Stores (NW) and Sinclair Stores (SE), which also stocks *Calor Gas*, each about 10 minutes' walk in opposite directions. Post office at Achiltibuie.

Tanera Mor: The Anchorage on the east side of the island is generally deep and obstructed by fish cages.

The Cabbage Patch, between Eilean Beag and Eilean Mor on the south side of the bay, is full of moorings, although a small boat might anchor close inshore.

There is a good modern pier where a boat might dry out for repairs. Water at the pier.

Acairseid Driseach at the northwest corner of Tanera Mor, on the east side of Eilean na Saile, is shoal and full of weed.

A drying rock lies in the middle of the south end of the inlet.

Stac Mhic Aonghais   Horse Island

Stac Mhic Aonghais (Angus Stac) 283° open to the south of Horse Island clears Iolla Beg

Acairseid Driseach from Tanera Mor

The approach from the south by Caolas Mhill Gharbh (and north of Eilean na Saile) is straightforward.

Tanera Beg has several sheltered anchorages on its northeast side, but these are noted as being subject to strong tide and thick kelp.

Approach from north, keeping ¼ cable off the west side of Eilean Fada Mor to avoid rocks submerged and awash on the west side of the channel.

Floats and fishing nets are laid in this channel.

From south it is possible, in quiet weather, to approach above half tide by the passage between the east end of Tanera Beg and Eilean Fada Mor, in which the least depth is charted as 0·8 metres with two rocks which dry 0·9 metres.

The passage between the drying rock in the middle of the south entrance and reefs at the south end of Eilean Fada Mor is only ½ cable wide.

Steer to pass ¼ cable from the east side of the passage, heading 360°, and as soon as the west end of the passage opens alter course to pass close northeast of the east point of Tanera Beg.

A line astern for this passage, Cailleach Head lighthouse over the left tangent of Eilean Dubh 170°, has been found to lead between the rocks in this passage.

Caolas Eilean Ristol, 58°02'·5N 5°25'·5W. Anchor off the slip clear of moorings, and show an anchor light as fishing boats come in after dark.

Light on end of the slip, Fl.G.3s.
Shop at Polbain, 2 miles.

Loch an Alltain Duibh, north of Eilean Ristol, provides occasional anchorage off the north shore of Eilean Ristol.

For passage notes see the beginning of this chapter.

Enard Bay
There are several moderately sheltered inlets on the east side of the bay, with offshore islands that give some further shelter, but none can be particularly recommended.

Charts
2504 (1:25,000)
OS map *15*

Tides
Streams are insignificant in Enard Bay.

Constant −0005 Ullapool (−0425 Dover)

Height in metres

MHWS	MHWN	MTL	MLWN	MLWS
5·0	3·9	3·0	2·1	0·8

Dangers and marks
Detached drying rocks lie up to 2 cables off the shore, both of the mainland and of various islands.

Loch an Eisg-Brachaidh from southeast

These are shown on chart *1794* but, for exploring, inshore chart *2504* must be used.

Eilean Mor, the highest island in Enard Bay, 4 miles east of Rubha Coigeach and ½ mile offshore, is a useful reference point.

Lights

Soyea Island (Loch Inver) Fl(2)10s34m6M
Stoerhead Fl.15s59m24M

Anchorages

Achnahaird Bay, 58°04'N 5°21'·5W, on the south side of Enard Bay, has a fine sandy beach, but is too exposed for all but an occasional daytime anchorage.

Camas a' Bhothain, 58°05'N 5°21'W, immediately east of Achnahaird Bay, is named Sandy Bay on old charts, but fails to live up to this name as the bottom consists of boulders and holding is poor.

A drying reef extends north from Rubha Beag at the west side of the bay towards Black Rock which dries, 1 cable north of a rock which does not cover, on the reef.

The entrance is between this reef and rocks which extend ½ cable west of Sgeir Bhuidhe in the middle of the bay.

Lochan Salainn, 58°05'N 5°17'W, is probably the best anchorage in Enard Bay. It is not named on some charts but lies about a mile southeast of Eilean Mor.

Islets extend northwest from its entrance to Sgeir Ghlas Mhor and Bheag which have drying rocks up to 1 cable north of them and a submerged rock ½ cable southeast.

A drying rock lies more than ½ cable from the northeast side of the inlet and there are some fish cages.

Loch an Eisg-Brachaidh, 58°06'·3N 5°16'·5W, ¾ mile east of Eilean Mor, is sheltered by several islands. Several rocks within are not shown on uncorrected copies of the current chart (see plan).

A drying rock lies ¾ cable southeast of Fraochlan, the island north of Eilean Mor, and more drying rocks lie in the middle of the passage north of Fraochlan.

Approach by either side of Eilean Mor but, if by the north side, keep closer to Eilean Mor.

Anchor close to the northeast side of Rubh a' Bhrocaire at the south side of the bay.

Loch Kirkaig, 58°07'·5N 5°17'W, ¾ mile southeast of Kirkaig Point at the entrance to Loch Inver, provides some shelter close to the south shore.

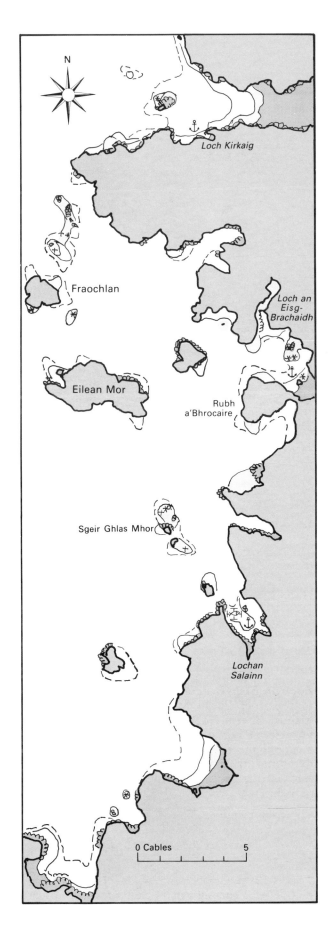

Enard Bay

Loch Inver
58°09'N 5°15'W

See colourphoto facing this page

A new breakwater provides good shelter, with pontoons for yachts up to 12 metres. The harbour is used by Breton fishing boats up to 50 metres in length.

Tides

Constant −0005 Ullapool (−0425 Dover)

Height in metres

MHWS	MHWN	MTL	MLWN	MLWS
5·0	3·9	3·0	2·1	0·8

Dangers and marks

Soyea Island lies ½ mile off the entrance to the loch.

A submerged rock lies 2 cables north of its east end at a depth of 0·2 metres and drying reefs up to 2 cables northeast of its east point.

Bo Caolas, which dries 3·2 metres, 3 cables northeast of the east point of the island, has a beacon with a cage topmark at its west end.

Glas Leac, 1¼ miles east of Soyea Island, is a small grass-topped islet 6 metres high with drying reefs and shoals up to ½ cable north of it.

Drying rocks lie more than a cable off the north shore north of Glas Leac, and off the east point of Camas na Frithearaich, ½ mile northwest of the islet.

Most of the bays on the south side of the loch are occupied by moorings and some have drying rocks in them.

Lights

Soyea Island Fl(2)10s34m6M
Glas Leac Fl.WRG.3s7m
Breakwater, Q.G.3m1M
Finger Jetty 2F.G(vert)
Pier head 2F.G(vert)

At night

Glas Leac light beacon shows white over the fairways, both north and south of Soyea Island, but the south passage is cleaner; a white sector also shows eastward towards the harbour.

Minor anchorages

Goat Pool, 58°08'·3N 5°17'W, ½ mile east of Kirkaig Point, is deep and the bottom is rocky until close in.

Pass either side of Bogh' an Tairbh which is only 0·3 metres high with drying reefs ½ cable east of it.

Loch Bad nam Ban, 58°08'·25N 5°16'·4W, has enough moorings to make it difficult to find space to anchor.

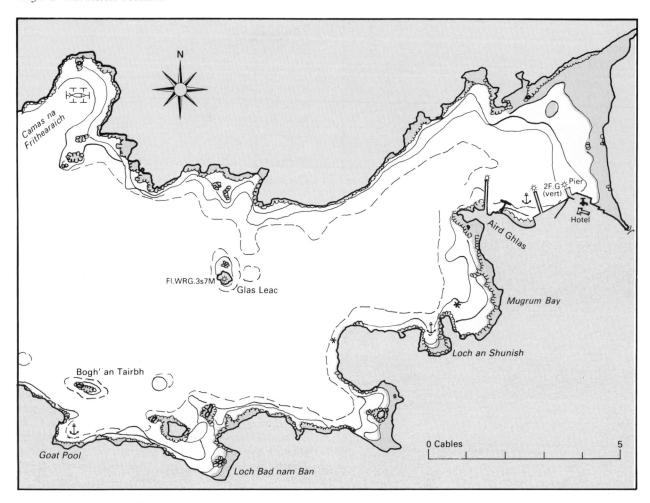

Lochinver Harbour

See colour photo facing page 107

The head of the new breakwater lies 6 cables east of Glas Leac.

Visiting yachts are requested to contact the harbourmaster by VHF before entering harbour. Watch is kept, although not 24hr, on Ch 16.

Pontoons are provided for small craft (up to 12 metres) between the breakwater and the Finger Jetty.

For those who prefer to anchor there may be space between the breakwater and the pontoons.

Yachts should not be left unattended alongside fixed jetties or quays. Wherever berthed, consult the harbourmaster immediately.

Supplies

Shops (shop at the pier open in evenings when fishing boats come in). Baker, post office, telephone, hotel. Petrol at garage, diesel and water at pier. Fishermen's chandlery; *Calor Gas* at chandlery. Harbourmaster has VHF. A concrete slip beyond the Culag Pier may be available to dry out for underwater repairs.

Loch Roe

58°10'N 5°18'W

The entrance lies 1 mile north of Soyea Island.
Pool Bay which provides the best shelter may be fully occupied by moorings.

Dangers and marks

Bo Burrick, ½ cable NNW of Rubha Rodha, the south point of the entrance, dries 4·1 metres,
   McAllister Rock ¼ cable off the north side of the entrance channel, dries 2·1 metres.

About 6 cables northeast of Rubha Rodha, two tidal islets, about 4 metres high, lie northeast of a promontory which extends northeast from the south shore, sheltering the anchorage at Pool Bay.
   Drying reefs extend 20–30 metres east of the islets.
   Bo Pool, which dries 1·7 metres, lies less than ½ cable further east.
   Submerged rocks may lie at the sides of the channel.
   Approach either when Bo Pool is showing or when the tide has risen enough to pass safely over it and anchor in Pool Bay, south of the islets.

East of Bo Pool a sill with drying rocks on it lies across the loch, but it is possible, with great care, to

Lochinver, small-craft pontoons from the new breakwater,
during a strong westerly wind

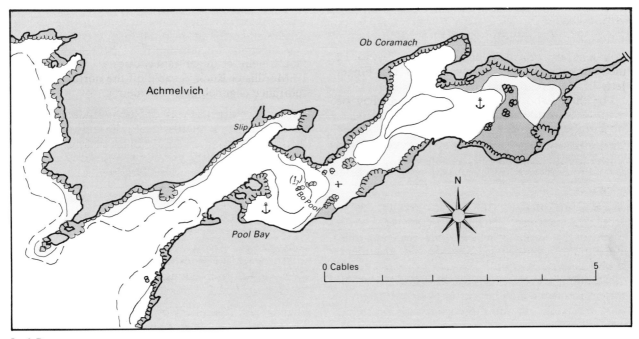

Loch Roe

Pool Bay, Loch Roe, from north.

pass further up the loch. Inshore fishing boats are moored in various inlets around the loch.

Eddrachillis Bay

Between Point of Stoer and Handa Island is an entertaining collection of islands and lochs, well worth the effort of getting there.

No general directions are necessary other than the passage notes on page 104 and a reminder of the heavy seas to be expected at Point of Stoer.

Charts
2502 (1:25,150) is essential for exploring the area in any detail
OS maps *15, 9*

Tides
Except in Kylesku, streams are insignificant in Eddrachillis Bay.

Constant 0000 Ullapool (−0420 Dover)

Height in metres

MHWS	MHWN	MTL	MLWN	MLWS
4·9	3·7	2·8	1·9	0·7

Anchorages
Clashnessie Bay, between Point of Stoer and Oldany Island, has no regular anchorage, but several bays and inlets might be rewarding to explore on a quiet day.

Culkein Drumbeg, 58°15'·2N 5°14'W, is a landlocked pool east of Oldany Island with rocks awash in the entrance which make the approach difficult, although they can often be seen breaking. Follow the plan closely.

Pass about a cable northeast of Eilean nan Uan and steer 160° as if to pass clear west of Eilean na Cille, but look out for the rock awash north of Eilean nam Boc.

When the north side of Eilean nam Boc comes abeam steer to starboard to pass ¼ cable off its east point and avoid the drying reef on the east side of the channel.

Hold on towards the south side of the inlet before turning east to avoid a rock which dries 3 metres southwest of Eilean na Cille and, if heading further east, keep towards one side or the other to avoid a rock which dries 0·9 metres in mid-channel.

The head of the jetty just dries. Water tap at jetty.

Loch Dhrombaig, 58°15'N 5°12'W, is straightforward to approach except for a submerged rock ½ cable west of the 15-metre islet north of the west entrance.

Anchor off shingle beach at the southeast side of the pool.

In the east entrance to the loch the least depth is 1·8 metres.

Submerged rocks lie 1 cable offshore ½ mile further east.

Drying rocks lie west and southwest of Sgeir Liath, the outermost islet northeast of Loch Dhrombaig.

Shop, post office, telephone, hotel. Advice and assistance may be sought from Drumbeg Charters at the hotel ☎ 015713 236.

Loch Nedd, 58°15'N 5°10'W, can be safely approached in heavy northerly weather and provides good shelter.

Drying reefs extend almost halfway across the entrance from the west side and up to a cable north of Rubha Dhubhard.

Many moorings lie in the inner loch and the head dries off for ¼ mile.

Loch Ardbhair, 58°15'N 5°07'W, is cluttered with rocks and even the outer part of this loch is occupied by fish cages and floats, but there is some space to anchor.

Pass east of the reef in the mouth of the loch, which does not usually cover, and anchor in the southwest corner of the outer loch.

Four cables beyond the reef at the entrance the loch is almost completely blocked by drying rocks where the tide runs strongly, although a way through can be found.

Further in, there are more fish cages.

South of an islet, another reef occupies most of the middle of the loch and the head of the loch dries off ¼ mile, but anyone who has penetrated thus far may find a clear anchorage under the west shore.

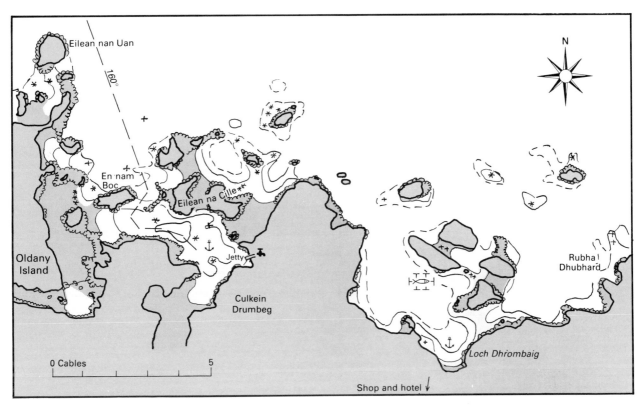

Drumbeg

Culkein Drumbeg from east.

Culkein Drumbeg entrance from southeast: a fishing boat is passing
out through the entrance channel at the left of the photo, and a rock
awash is showing off the north point of Eilean nam Boc

Loch Dhrombaig from west

Loch Nedd

Poll a' Ghamhna, with Kylesku Bridge showing beyond Eilean a'
Ghamhna. The dark object at the right is a fish cage

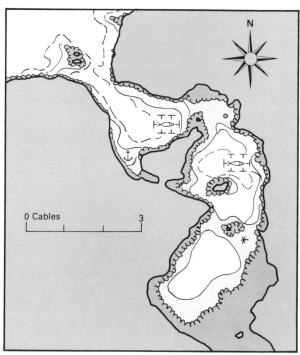

Loch Ardbhair

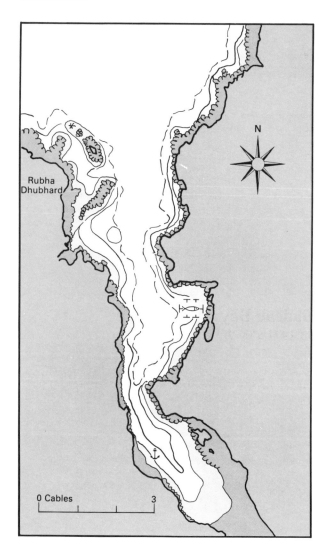

Loch Nedd

Loch a' Chairn Bhain

58°16'·5N 5°07'W

This loch is entered between Rubha nam Fias, on the south shore 5 miles east of Oldany Island, and the Calbha islands.

Ravens Rock, ¼ mile south of Calbha Beag, dries 1·8 metres and Lachen Shoal 4 cables WSW of Calbha Beag, at a depth of 2·1 metres, breaks heavily in gales.

Several inlets on the north side of the entrance remain unexplored.

Loch Shark, 58°16'·8N 5°06'·3W, the most easterly of these, has a submerged rock in the middle of its entrance, which is only ¼ cable wide.

Kerrachar Bay, 4 cables SSE of Rubha na Fias, is an occasional anchorage, off a house on the shore. Reefs extend more than ½ cable from the north point of the bay, there are fish cages, and the bottom has been found to be thick with weed.

Loch a' Chairn Bhain runs in a southeasterly direction for 4 miles to Kylesku (Caolas Cumhann) a narrow passage where the tide runs strongly with eddies on each side. An elegant concrete bridge and power cables cross the narrows, both with 24 metres headroom.

Tides

At Kylesku tides run at up to 2h knots

The in-going stream begins −0545 Ullapool (+0220 Dover)

The out-going stream begins +0040 Ullapool (−0340 Dover)

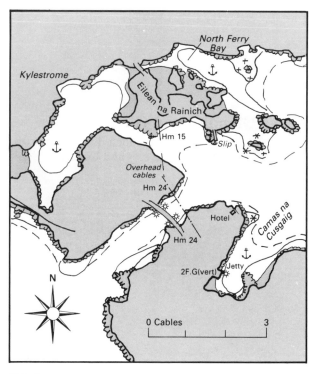

Kylesku

Lights

Q.R.24m3M lights are shown from the north bridge supports on both sides, and Q.G.24m3M from the south bridge supports.

Poll a' Ghamhna, south of Eilean a' Ghamhna, 1 mile west of Kylesku is rather deep until close inshore, and the head of the bay dries off ½ cable.

A shoal spit extends ½ cable south from the southeast point of the island.

Kylestrome A pool north of Garbh Eilean on the north side of Kylesku is entered by a narrow channel northeast of Garbh Eilean across which runs a power cable with headroom of 15 metres.

Reefs extend more than halfway across the entrance channel from the north side leaving a passage perhaps no more than 20 metres wide; keep close to the southwest shore at the point where the channel narrows.

North Ferry Bay, north of Eilean na Rainich, is entered by the east and north sides of that island.

Drying and submerged rocks extend 1 cable from the north shore of the inlet and there are some fishing boat moorings.

Camas na Cusgaig (South Ferry Bay), south of the east point of the narrows, has several moorings.

A concrete fishing jetty stands at the northwest side of the head of the inlet.

A drying rock lies ¼ cable offshore at the north side of the entrance and, although this sounds close enough to the shore, it can catch a stranger coming round the corner.

A large can buoy marks the outer limit of discarded moorings.

Lights

2F.G(vert) are shown at the jetty.

Supplies

Post office, telephone, hotel. Petrol and diesel at hotel by south ferry slip, water at jetty.

Lochs Glendhu and Glencoul

Two miles east of Kylesku the loch divides into two parts: Loch Glendhu to the east and Loch Glencoul to the southeast.

Loch Glendhu is clean with moderate depths at the head. Loch Glencoul has several hazards.

In its outer part the northeast shore is clean but, on the southwest side, a drying rock lies ¼ cable east of Eilean a Choin a' Chreige, the island furthest from the shore.

Another rock which dries 0·3 metres lies 2 cables southeast of the same island.

Loch Beag A narrow passage leads southwest of a group of islands, of which the largest is Eilean Ard, to Loch Beag.

A drying reef extends northeast from Eilean an Tuim at the west side of the narrows; hold towards

the island north of Eilean Ard and then keep midway between the next island and the south shore.

A drying rock, which does not appear on some charts, lies south of the east end of this island.

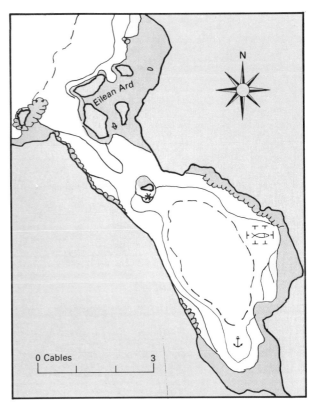

Loch Beag

Anchorages North of Kylesku

Calbha Bay, 58°17'N 5°07'·5W, east of Calbha Mor, has fish cages along its west shore. Should these later be moved to the east side (fish cages are moved around to find cleaner water), care will be needed to avoid a reef which dries 3·1 metres extending about 1 cable from the west side.

Badcall Bay

58°19'N 5°09'W
See colour photo facing page 106

A well-sheltered anchorage behind a dense group of islands on the east side of Eddrachillis Bay. A large number of fish cages lies on the southeast side of the bay.

Tides

Constant +0005 Ullapool (−0415 Dover)

Height in metres

MHWS	MHWN	MTL	MLWN	MLWS
4·5	3·4	2·6	1·6	0·9

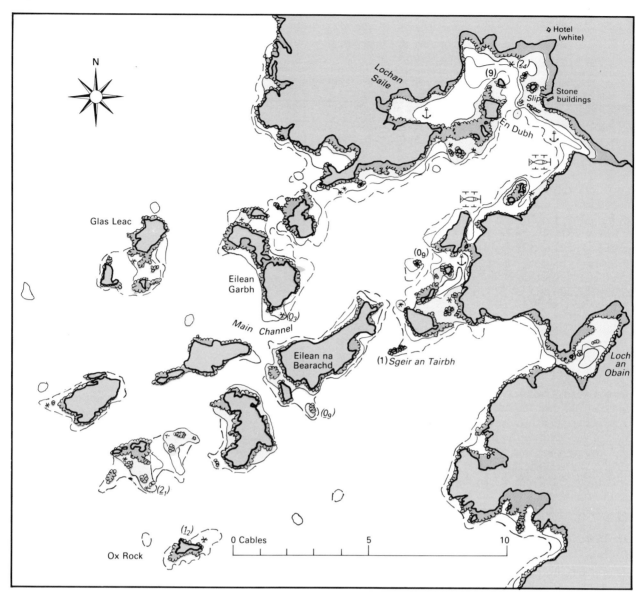

Badcall Islands

Approach

From south, a possible hazard is a rock which dries 0·9 metres 1 cable south of Eilean na Bearachd.

South Channel lies east of Eilean na Bearachd, and west of Sgeir an Tairbh which is 1 metre high. At the northeast end of Eilean na Bearachd, keep in mid-channel as reefs and drying rocks extend from either side.

Continue north for 2 cables until past a rock 0·9 metres high to starboard, and then head northeast.

Main Channel leads north of Ceannamhor and Eilean na Bearachd.

A submerged rock lies a cable north of Ceannamhor at a depth of 1·8 metres, and a rock which dries 0·3 metres lies ¼ cable south of Eilean Garbh.

From north, pass between Glas Leac and Eilean Garbh and enter by Main Channel.

Lochan Saile on the north side of Badcall Bay is sheltered by islands and drying reefs. The bottom consists of soft mud and care should be taken that the anchor is well dug in.

To enter from Badcall Bay, pass ¼ – ½ cable east of Eilean Dubh to avoid reefs extending east from the island, as well as drying and submerged rocks on the east side of the passage.

Pass east and north of the 9-metre islet north of Eilean Dubh and anchor in the western part of the bay.

Supplies

Water at slip on the east side of the passage to Lochan Saile. Hotel in the northeast corner, otherwise none (but see Scourie, below).

Scourie

58°21'N 5°10'W

This is the only source of stores between Lochinver

The head of Scourie Bay from southwest

and Kinlochbervie, apart from a small shop at Drumbeg. Scourie Bay is completely exposed, with several submerged and drying rocks in the entrance. If in doubt, go shopping by land from Badcall, about 3 miles by road.

Supplies

Shop, post office, telephone, hotel. Petrol, diesel and *Calor Gas* at garage.

Handa, Loch Laxford and Loch Inchard

Charts

2503 (1:25,000)

OS map *9*

Handa Sound

58°23'N 5°10'W

Handa Island is an RSPB reserve with a resident warden.

Tides

Tidal streams in the sound run at up to 3 knots.

The north-going stream begins −0405 Ullapool (+0400 Dover)

The south-going stream begins +0220 Ullapool (−0200 Dover)

Dangers and marks

Bodha Morair, in mid-channel in Handa Sound at a depth of 1·8 metres, causes heavy overfalls.

At the north end of the sound a drying reef extends 1 cable from Roinn Dubh on Handa, and Bodha Iasg lies in mid-channel at a depth of 1·6 metres.

Sgeir Bellaire, 1 metre high, lies on the northeast side of the passage, 1 cable south of Eilean an

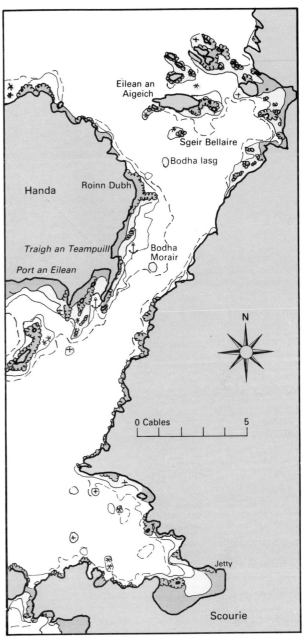

Handa Sound and Scourie Bay

Aigeich, the largest and highest island in the north channel.

Occasional anchorages

Traigh an Teampuill on the east side of Handa, as close inshore as depth allows.

Port an Eilean at the southeast of the island. Approach from SSW; there are no clearing marks for the rocks on either side of the entrance.

Loch Laxford

58°25'N 5°07'W

See colour photo facing page 107

Much of the land around the loch is bare reddish-coloured rock, with a little heather growing on peat

Handa Sound from northeast. Traigh an Teampuill, Handa, is on the right, and Point of Stoer on the horizon with the Old Man of Stoer beside it

in the hollows. The shores are broken and indented to an extraordinary extent and many anchorages can be found with the large-scale chart, although several of them contain fish cages.

Tides

Streams in the loch are insignificant.

Constant +0015 Ullapool (−0405 Dover)

Height in metres

MHWS	MHWN	MTL	MLWN	MLWS
4·9	3·5	2·8	1·9	0·7

Directions

The entrance, 2 miles northeast of Handa, is clean and straightforward, as is the fairway.

There are no lights and no supplies are available nearer than Scourie, which is about 5 miles by road from Foindle.

Anchorages

Crow Harbour (Fanagmore), 58°24'N 5°07'W, is the first anchorage on the south side on entering the loch.

Pass north and east of Eilean Ard ('69' on chart *1785*), the largest and highest island in the loch, although even with only the small-scale chart it would be possible to cautiously thread a way through among the outer islands.

The principal hazard here is a drying rock 1 cable southwest of Sgeir Iosal which is 3½ cables WNW of Eilean Ard.

Although there is an extensive fish farm in the anchorage swinging room can still be found. Anchor on the west side, off the jetty.

Foindle Bay (58°23'·8N 5°05'W), Bagh na Fionndalach Moire on the chart, about a mile ESE of Crow Harbour, is rather deep and the sides shelve steeply.

Enter by the north and east side of Eilean a Mhadaidh.

Weaver's Bay, 58°23'N 5°04'W, nearly a mile southeast of Foindle Bay, provides the best shelter in moderate depths of any bay on the south side of the loch.

Nearest supplies are at Scourie.

Loch a' Chadh-fi, 58°24'·5N 5°04'W, on the northeast side of the loch is entered by the east side of Eilean an Eireannaich (61 metres).

A rock which dries 2·8 metres lies ½ cable from the southeast shore 3 cables within the loch.

Eilean a' Chadh-fi lies in mid-channel about ¾ mile inside the loch. The deeper and broader channel is west and north of the island, but the west side of the loch is full of fish cages and moorings.

Hazards north of the island are avoided by keeping ½ cable off its shore.

Anchor north of the island, or anywhere in the upper part of the loch, but the head is shoal for about ¼ mile.

Several other anchorages may be found in Loch Laxford with the large-scale chart.

B.Spenue	Ru Ruag	Fonnbhein	Arkle	Stack of Laxford

Loch Inchard

58°27'·5N 5°05'W

Tides

Constant +0020 Ullapool (−0400 Dover)

Height in metres

MHWS	MHWN	MTL	MLWN	MLWS
4·9	3·6	2·8	1·9	0·7

Dangers and marks

Dubh Sgeirean is a group of islands about a mile offshore between Loch Laxford and Loch Inchard with a channel ½ mile wide between them and Sgeirean Cruaidhe nearer the shore.

Whale Back, which dries 3·8 metres southwest of Dubh Sgeirean is usually breaking.

Sgeir Geinn, 1½ cables west of the most southerly of Sgeirean Cruaidhe is awash at HW.

The most northerly of Sgeirean Cruaidhe is 8 metres high, which is not clear from chart *1785*, and Sgeir an Daimh, 3 metres high, lies 3 cables northwest of it.

The passage inshore of Dubh Sgeirean and east of Sgeir an Daimh can usually be taken.

Glas Leac, two islets at the south side of the entrance to Loch Inchard joined at low water, have a clear deep passage more than ½ cable wide inshore of them, but 3-metre patches 1½ cables southwest of them might cause a bad breaking sea if much swell is running.

Eilean an Roin Beag, 2 miles northwest of the mouth of Loch Inchard, is the most southwesterly point of land northwest of the approach to the loch.

Bodha Roin, nearly a cable southwest of the island, dries 0·7 metre.

Kinsale Rock (Bodha Ceann na Saile), 4 cables within the entrance just south of mid-channel at a depth of 3 metres, breaks if a swell is running. The southern extremity of the north shore of the loch in line with the south shore of Loch Sheigra ahead 098° leads north of Kinsale Rock.

Lights

Rubha na Leacaig on the north side of the entrance Fl(2)10s30m8M

Cape Wrath lighthouse, Fl(4)30s122m24M, is obscured east of about 025°, or the line of the coast north of Eilean an Roin Beag

Loch Bervie (Kinlochbervie)

58°27'·5N 5°03'W

The third-largest fishing harbour in Scotland by volume of fish landed, this is often too busy for a visiting yacht to find space although a pontoon has been provided for small craft in the NNE corner.

Yachts should make a brief visit for supplies (dues

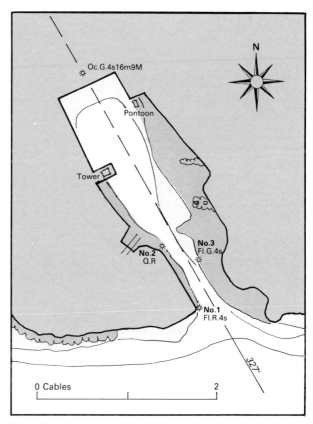

Kinlochbervie

are charged for even a brief stay) and anchor overnight elsewhere.

The entrance is dredged between drying banks marked by light beacons, but take note of the spit on the east side extending west, well north of the beacon on that side.

Leading beacons at the head of the harbour, framework towers with topmarks consisting of orange triangles on white squares, bearing 327°, lead into the harbour.

Loch Bervie from the northeast shore. The small-boat pontoon is at the bottom right

Entrance to Kinlochbervie at low tide

A beacon on the south shore of Loch Inchard, *Creag Mhor*, provides a white light sector 1° wide bearing 146°.

Lights

Ldg lights 327° *Front* Oc.G.8s9M *Rear* 330m from front Oc.G.8s26m9M
No. 1 beacon Fl.R.4s
No. 2 beacon Q.R
No. 3 beacon Fl.G.4s
Creag Mhor, OcWRG.2·8s16m9M

Radio

VHF Ch 12, 16

Services and supplies

Shop (uphill from the harbour), post office, telephone, hotel.

Showers may be available at the Royal National Mission to Deep Sea Fishermen (not weekends).

Petrol at garage. Diesel and water at quay, *Calor Gas*.

Fishermen's chandlery, mechanical, electronic, hull repairs.

Minor anchorages

Mol Bhain (Camas Blair) on the south shore ½ mile southwest of the entrance to Loch Bervie.

Anchor ½ cable off the southwest shore; subject to swell and wash from passing traffic (there may be a fish farm by now).

Loch Sheigra, 58°27'N 5°01'W, 1 mile east of Loch Bervie, is mostly shoal and drying, but has a depth of 2 metres 1 cable within the entrance.

Stores at Badcall on the north shore.

Achriesgill Bay, 1 mile further southeast, dries at the head and the bottom drops steeply to more than 15 metres.

Rhiconich, 58°26'N 5°00'W, at the head of the loch. The water in the middle is shoal for about ½ mile from the head of the loch, but deeper on either side. Hotel, post office, telephone, garage.

Anchorages North of Loch Inchard

Loch Clash, 58°27'·7N 5°04'W, is open to the west and used by fishing boats for landing their catches but, in quiet weather, is an alternative to entering Loch Bervie for stores.

Coastal passage to Cape Wrath

Cape Wrath is 10 miles from Eilean an Roin Beag and there is no secure shelter eastward nearer than Loch Eriboll, a further 14 miles.

Dangers and marks

Eilean an Roin Beag – Dubh Sgeir, 10 metres high, lies ½ mile north of Eilean an Roin Beag and rocks above water and drying lie between Dubh Sgeir and the coast ½ mile NNE.

Am Balg, 44 metres high, lies a mile offshore 4 miles north of Eilean an Roin Beag with drying rocks up to 2 cables from it.

Waypoint 1 mile west of Am Balg 57°33'N 5°09'W

Duslic Rock, which dries 3·4 metres, lies 7 cables NNE of Cape Wrath. Am Balg just open northwest of Cape Wrath 215° leads west of Duslic Rock.

Tides

Tidal streams reach 1¾ knots at springs.

The north-going stream begins −0110 Ullapool (−0530 Dover).

The south-going stream begins +0505 Ullapool (+0045 Dover).

It is noted that a south-going eddy runs ½–¾ miles offshore during the north-going tide.

Appendix

I. CHARTS AND OTHER PUBLICATIONS

Imray charts – Imray's *C65*, *C66* and *C67*, at a scale of about 1:150,000, cover the waters referred to in this volume. They are available at most chandlers and from the Clyde Cruising Club, usually folded, but for any boat which has a large enough chart table it is better to order a flat copy.

A general chart for the whole west coast of Scotland is Admiralty chart *2635* at a scale of 1:500,000.

The following Admiralty charts relate to the waters covered by this volume. Some of these are essential and, the more you have, the less your pilotage will be fraught with anxiety. The relevant Ordnance Survey maps are also listed.

Chart	Title – areas in Chapters I and II	Scale
2207	Ardnamurchan to Sound of Sleat	1:50,000
2208	Mallaig to Canna Harbour	1:50,000
OS 39	Small Isles	1:50,000
OS 40	Mallaig	1:50,000

Chart	Title – areas in Chapter III	Scale
2208	Mallaig to Canna Harbour	1:50,000
1795	The Little Minch	1:100,000
2533	Lochs Dunvegan and Snizort	1:25,000
OS 32	South Skye	1:50,000
OS 23	North Skye	1:50,000

Chart	Title – areas in Chapter IV	Scale
2208	Mallaig to Canna Harbour	1:50,000
2209	Inner Sound	1:50,000
2541	Lochs Nevis, Hourn and Duich	1:25,000
2540	Loch Alsh	1:25,000
OS 33	Loch Alsh and Glen Shiel	1:50,000

Chart	Title – areas in Chapter V	Scale
2209	Inner Sound	1:50,000
2210	Approaches to Inner Sound	1:50,000
2534	Plans in the Inner Sound	1:25,000
2528	Loch Carron and Loch Gairloch	1:25,000
2498	Inner Sound, Southern Part	1:25,000
2479	Inner Sound, Middle Part	1:18,000
2480	Inner Sound, Northern Part	1:25,000
OS 33	Loch Alsh and Glen Shiel	1:50,000
OS 24	Raasay and Loch Torridon	1:50,000

Chart	Title – areas in Chapter VI	Scale
1785	North Minch, Northern Part	1:100,000
1794	North Minch, Southern Part	1:100,000
2509	Rubha Reidh to Cailleach Head	1:25,000
2500	Loch Broom and Approaches	1:25,000
2501	Summer Isles	1:26,000
2502	Eddrachillis Bay	1:25,150
2503	Lochs Laxford and Inchard	1:25,000
2504	Approaches to Loch Inver	1:25,000
3146	Loch Ewe	1:12,500
OS 19	Gairloch and Ullapool	1:50,000
OS 15	Loch Assynt	1:50,000
OS 9	Cape Wrath	1:50,000

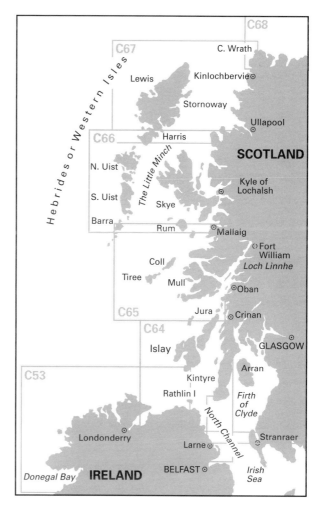

Imray chart coverage

OS Outdoor Leisure Map – The Cuillin and Torridon Hills (1:25,000) provides much more detail, especially for southwest Skye and the southwest side of the Inner Sound, than a chart is able to do.

The Simpson Lawrence Yachtsman's Almanac – North and West Britain, published annually, is available from chandlers or post free from the publishers, Clyde Marine Press, Westgate, Toward, Argyll PA23 7UA.

There are Admiralty chart agents throughout Britain, and in most other countries. Chart agents on the West Coast are:

Kelvin Hughes, Glasgow ☎ 0141 221 5452
Christie and Wilson, Glasgow ☎ 0141 552 7137
Johnston Brothers, Mallaig ☎ 01687 2215
Ullasport, Ullapool ☎ 01854 2621

Imray, Laurie, Norie & Wilson Ltd is an Admiralty chart agent and will supply charts by post. Address: Wych House, The Broadway, St Ives, Huntingdon,

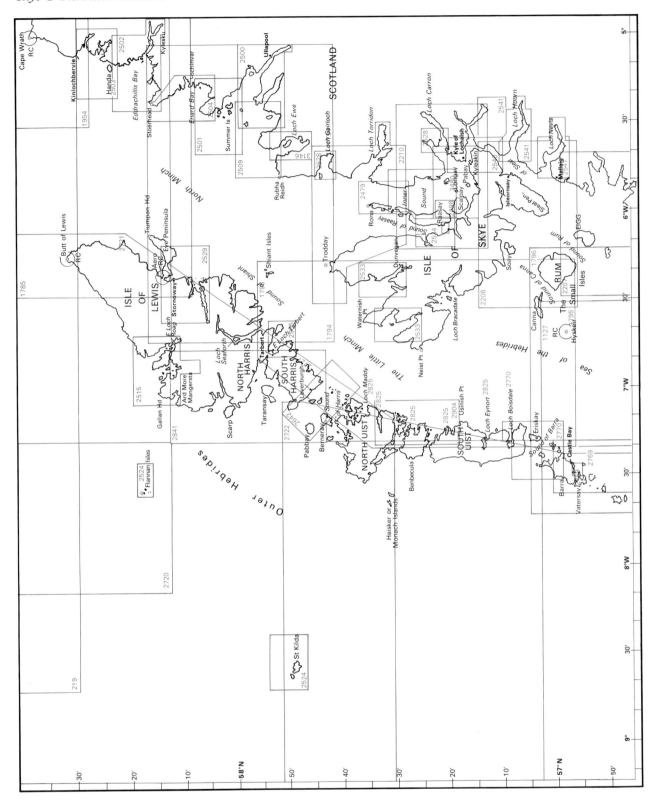

Cambridgeshire PE17 4BT ☎ 01480 62114, *Fax* 01480 496109. They can also arrange for charts to be laminated.

Some charts which have long been discontinued provide much more detail, at a larger scale, than any now published for the same area. All older charts, particularly the fine Victorian engravings, show more detail inshore and on land than the current publications, although they may be less accurate. Old charts should only be used to supplement current ones, not as a substitute for them.

The following old charts, in particular, may be found useful:

531	Loch Moidart	1:7900
2817	Loch na Ceall	1:10700
2638	Loch Torridon	1:25000

Photocopies of old charts – of editions not less than 50 years old, for copyright reasons – may be obtained from the National Library of Scotland Map Room Annexe, 33 Salisbury Place, Edinburgh 9 ☎ 0131 226 4531.

Current charts show less detail ashore than older charts, and Ordnance Survey maps at a scale of 1:50,000, or Bartholomew maps at 1:100,000 help to fill in the picture.

A set of 50 sketch charts published by the Clyde Cruising Club (CCC) is available from chandlers or direct from the CCC at Suite 408, The Pentagon Centre, Washington Street, Glasgow G3 8AZ ☎ 0141 221 2774 *Fax* 0141 221 2775. These charts are convenient to use because of their size, but the relevant Admiralty charts should also be carried.

The *Clyde Cruising Club Sailing Directions and Anchorages* are also available from the CCC at the above address.

The new edition of the *Admiralty West Coast of Scotland Pilot* (NP 66), is a most valuable publication. New editions of *Admiralty Pilots* are now published every three years or so without regular supplements, but any important corrections are published in *Weekly Notices to Mariners*.

The *Admiralty Tidal Stream Atlas* for the North Coast of Ireland and West Coast of Scotland (NP 218) is very useful.

Tide tables are essential, preferably for Ullapool, giving heights of each high and low water.

Pilotage books

Scottish West Coast Pilot, Mark Brackenbury, Stanford 1981
Ardnamurchan to Cape Wrath Sailing Directions, Clyde Cruising Club, 1984

General books

The Scottish Islands, by Hamish Haswell Smith, is an extremely useful general guide, published by Canongate in 1996
Exploring Scotland's Heritage – The Highlands, Joanna Close-Brooks, HMSO 1986
The Islands of Scotland including Skye, Scottish Mountaineering Trust, 1989 (for climbers and hillwalkers)

II. SUBMARINE EXERCISE AREAS

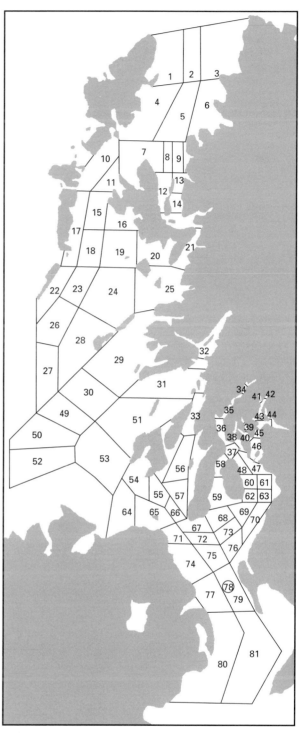

Scottish eubmarine exercise areas including SUBFACTS. SUBFACTS may also be obtained from COMCLYDE using the 'Fishermans' Hotline', ☎ 0374 613097

Transmissions of:

0060	Anglesey	0062	Morecambe Bay
0121	Belfast CG	0074	Oban
0085	Buchan	0075	Oban CG
0059	Cardigan Bay	0081	Orkney
0088	Cullercoats (GCC)	0065	Portpatrick (GPK)
0070	Clyde	0082	Shetland
0072	Clyde CG	0076	Skye
0087	Forth	0086	Stonehaven (GND)
0077	Hebrides (GHD	0079	Stornoway CG
0073	Islay	0093	Whitby
0078	Lewis	0080	Wick (GKR)

1. Tiumpan X5816
2. Minch North X5817
3. Stoer X5818
4. Shiant X5815
5. Minch South X5814
6. Ewe X5813
7. Trodday X5715
8. Rona West X5716
9. Rona North X5717
10. Lochmaddy X5713
11. Dunvegan X5714
12. Portree X5720
13. Rona South X5718
14. Raasay XZ5719
15. Neist X5711
16. Bracadale X5709
17. Ushenish X5712
18. Hebrides North X5710
19. Canna X5708
20. Rhum X5707
21. Sleat X5706
22. Barra X5633
23. Hebrides Central X5632
24. Hawes X5635
25. Eigg X5636
26. Hebrides South X5631
27. Ford X5630
28. Tiree X5634
29. Staffa X5627
30. Mackenzie X5626
31. Mull X5628
32. Linnhe X5624
33. Jura Sound X5623
34. Fyne X5603
35. Minard X5602
36. Tarbert X5517
37. Skipness X5516
38. West Kyle X5518
39. Striven X5520
40. East Kyle X5519
41. Goll X5604
42. Long X5606
43. Cove M5605
44. Gareloch X5620
45. Rosneath X5506
46. Cumbrae X5507
47. Garroch X5508
48. Laggan X5509
49. Blackstone X5542
50. Place X5541
51. Colonsay X5543
52. Boyle X5540
53. Orsay X5539
54. Islay X5538
55. Otter X5535
56. Gigha X5534
57. Earadale X5533
58. Lochranza X5515
59. Davaar X5514
60. Brodick X5510
61. Irvine X5511
62. Lamlash X5513
63. Ayr X5512
64. Skerries X5537
65. Rathlin X5536
66. Kintyre X5531
67. Sanda X5530
68. Stafnish X5523
69. Pladda X5522
70. Turnberry X5521
71. Torr X5528
72. Mermaid X5529
73. Ailsa X5524
74. Maiden X5529
75. Corsewall X5526
76. Ballantrae X5525
77. Magee X5407
78. Londonderry X5401
79. Beaufort X5408
80. Ardglass X5402
81. Peel X5403

III. QUICK REFERENCE TABLE OF PROVISIONS, SERVICES AND SUPPLIES

Columns

1	Water	A	Alongside, by hose
		T	Tap on jetty or quay
		N	Nearby tap
2	Shop	S	Several, or supermarket
		L	Local, well stocked village store
		B	Basic
3	Diesel	A	Alongside, by hose
		M	Marine diesel, near
		G	Garage
4	Petrol	P	(usually needs to be carried some distance)
5	Calor Gas	C	
6	Repairs	H	Hull
		M	Marine engine
		E	Electronics (engineer may need to come from a distance)
7	Chandlery	Y	Yacht
		F	Fishermen's chandlery
		I	Ironmonger, hardware store, which may be better than nothing
8	Visitors' moorings	V	(including those provided by hotel for customers)
		P	Pontoon
9	Conveniences	R	Restaurant
		B	Bar
		S	Showers
10	Bank	£	
11	Rubbish disposal	D	

Page	Place, grouped in sequence of chapters	1	2	3	4	5	6	7	8	9	10	11
16	Glenuig		L	½						RB		
21	Arisaig harbour	A	L	M	P	C		(F)	V	RB		
26	Morar			L	G	P				RB		
27	Mallaig	A	S	D	P	C	HME	YF		RB	£	D
34	Eigg		L2			C						
48	Loch Harport:											
48	Loch Beg	L		RB								
48	Portnalong		L¾		RB							
48	Carbost	N	L			RB						
52	Dunvegan	S	G	P	C	F	I	V	RBS	D		
55	Stein			B		ME	Y	V	RBS			
55	Edinbane		S	G	P			RB				
57	Uig	T	L	G	P	HMED						
61	Inverie		L	RB								
63	Armadale	T	L	M		HM	V	RB	D			
64	Isleornsay	N	B	P		RB						

Page	Place, grouped in sequence of chapters	1	2	3	4	5	6	7	8	9	10	11
68	Glenelg	L	P	C		RB						
71	Dornie		S	P	C		RB					
71	Kyle Akin	A	S	G	P	C	RBS	D				
73	Kyle of Lochalsh	A	S	G	P	C	F	1(Y)	RBS	£	D	
76	Ardarroch	L	G	P			.					
76	Plockton	(A)G	S	M	C			RBS				
78	Lochcarron	S	G	P	C	I	RB	D				
81	Poll Creadha		B	P			.					
87	Shieldaig		S	C		RB	D					
87	Torridon	L				RB						
88	Badachro	A	L	A			Y	V	RBS	D		
88	Gairloch	A	S1	G1	P1	C	M		RB	£	D	
90	Broadford	S	G	P			RB					
94	Portree	A	S	M	P	C	M	YFI	V	RB	£	D
100	Staffin	L		.								
105	Aultbea	T	S		p	C	(ME)	RB				
105	Poolewe	L	G	P	C	RB						
107	Ullapool	A	S	A	P	C	ME	YFI	RB	£	D	
108	Achiltibuie	S		RB								
111	Loch Inver	A	S	A	P	C	RB	D				
114	Drumbeg	T	B				RB					
119	Kylesku	T	L	A	P		RB					
120	Scourie	L	P		RB							
123	Kinlochbervie	A	S	A	P	C	HME	F	RBS	D		

Notes

Figures following reference letter indicate the distance in miles from the landing place.

Caley Marine at Inverness ☎ 01463 236539 operates a mobile repair service.

IV GLOSSARY OF GAELIC WORDS WHICH COMMONLY APPEAR IN PLACE NAMES

Many varieties of spelling are found, so it is as well to search for possible alternatives; variations of the same word are listed together but usually at least have the same initial letter. Many words beginning with a consonant take an 'h' after the initial letter in certain cases; notably in adjectives the genitive and the feminine gender and genitive cases of nouns, so that most of the words below could have an 'h' as the second letter.

There is no possibility of guiding the reader on pronunciation except to say that consonants followed by an 'h' are not often pronounced, and that 'mh' and 'bh' at the beginning of a word are pronounced as (and of course in anglicised versions often spelt with) a 'v'. *Mhor* is pronounced – approximately – *vore*; *claidheamh* is something like *clayeh*, and *bogha* is *bo'a*.

Some names, particularly those of islands ending in 'a' or 'ay', are of Norse origin. Anyone at all familiar with French and Latin will see correspondences there, for example Caisteil – also Eaglais and Teampuill.

Many words are compounds made up of several often quite common parts, frequently linked by *na/nam/nan*. The following are the most usual forms of words which commonly occur in Gaelic place names. They often set out to describe the physical features and so give some clues to identification. Some of them occur almost everywhere; most lochs have a Sgeir More and an Eilean Dubh, or vice versa.

Gaelic	*English*
a, am, an, an t-	the
abhainn (avon)	river
acairseid	harbour (acair = anchor)
achadh (ach, auch)	field
allt	stream, burn
ard, aird	promontory
aros	house
ba	cattle
bairneach	limpet
bagh ('bay')	bay
ban	white, pale; female (ban-righ = queen), as noun: woman
bealach	narrow passage
beg, beag, beaga	small
ben, beinn	mountain
beul (bel)	mouth of (belnahua = mouth of the cave)
bodach	old man
bogha (bo')	a detached rock, usually one which uncovers
breac	speckled (as noun: trout)
buachaille	shepherd
buidhe (bhuidhe, buie)	yellow (also: pleasing)
bun	mouth of a river
cailleach	old woman
caisteil	castle
camas	bay
caol (a' chaolais)	narrow passage (kyle)

caorach	sheep
ceall, cille (kil...)	monastic cell, church
ceann (kin...)	head
clachan	usually a group of houses (clach = stone)
claidheamh	sword (hence 'claymore' = great sword)
cnoc (knock)	rounded hill
coire (corrie)	cauldron, hollow among hills, whirlpool
craobh	tree
creag	cliff, rock (crag)
darroch	oak tree
dearg ('jerrig')	red
deas	south
dobhran	otter
donn	brown (dun)
druim	ridge
dubh (dhu)	black, dark, (disastrous)
dun, duin	fortified place, usually prehistoric
each	horse
ear	east
eilean (or eileach)	island
fada	long
fir, fear	man
fraoch, fraoich	heather
garbh	rough
geal	white
gille	boy
glas	grey (sometimes green)
gobhar (gour)	goat (gabhar = she-goat)
gorm	blue
gamhna	stirk, year-old calf
iar	west (easily confused with Ear)
iolair	eagle
keills, kells	church
kin... (ceann)	head of
liath	grey
mara	sea
meadhonach	middle-sized
meall	lump, knob
mor (more, mhor, vore)	large, great (often only relative)
muc, muck	pig (often a sea-pig = porpoise or a whale)
na, na h-, nam, nan of (the)naomh (nave, neave)	holy, saint
...nish (ness)	point of land
poll, puill	pool
righ ('ree')	king
ron, roin	seal
ruadh, rudha	red, reddish
rubha (rhu)	point of land, promontory
sailean	creek
sgeir, sgeirean (skerry)	rock, above water or covering
sron	nose (as a headland)
sruth	stream, current
tigh	house
tober	well
traigh	beach
tuath (or tuadh)	north
uamh	cave

Index